DATE DUE

Demco, Inc. 38-293

DAYS OF MY LIFE

The Author, 1909

DAYS OF MY LIFE

MEMORIES OF
A KANSAS MOTHER
AND TEACHER

by

FLO V. MENNINGER

RICHARD R. SMITH
NEW YORK   1939

PRINTED IN THE UNITED STATES OF AMERICA
BY J. J. LITTLE AND IVES COMPANY, NEW YORK

With affection and gratitude
I dedicate this book
to

MY FAMILY

FOREWORD

AS far back as I can remember, I have had great
ambitions. One of these was to be able to write
well, but most of my writing has been letters to
absent members of my family and to my friends.
I would not have thought of writing up the experiences of my childhood had it not been for the encouragement of an old friend, herself an author,
whom I was visiting one day over forty years ago.
I was telling Mrs. Jessie Wright Whitcomb some
incidents in my early life, and she expressed great
interest in them and urged me to write them down
for my children to read someday. She herself wrote
several articles about my experiences for *The
Youth's Companion.*

I thought over her suggestion for some time and
then acted on it, not because I considered that my
life had been remarkable, but because I knew that
it had been very different from that of my children
and hence might prove interesting to them. I really
wrote it down for them to read.

Most of what follows was written during the
summer of 1899, while I was waiting for the day
that brought to our home my youngest son, William
Claire. I read what I had written to Mrs. Ella W.

Brown, a friend since my Holton, Kansas, days, who had stopped in to see me as she was passing through the city. I had typed the story myself and then retyped part of it and, after reading it to her, I put the manuscript—still in rough draft—in an unlabeled envelope, laid it aside and forgot it.

Twenty years later, we sold our old home at 1251 Topeka Avenue. In disposing of various things, I came across the envelope, looked into it and remembered the story written so long ago. It occurred to me that I might take it with me when I went to see my mother in Industry, so that if I did not have all the facts set down correctly, she could straighten them out for me. I laid the manuscript aside for the time being, but in the disturbance of moving, I forgot my good intentions and again the material was mislaid.

About two years later, I had a letter from Mrs. Brown, asking what I had done with the story I had read to her so long ago. She wrote, "As I remember it, it sounded much like the reading material *The Atlantic Monthly* is sending out these days." I showed her letter to my son Karl, and he and his brothers were eager to see what I had written, so I tried to think what I had done with the manuscript. I spent a week looking for it among everything I had kept from the ash heap. Just when I had given it up for lost, I happened to be in the barn loft, looking through a box of pictures I had saved to give to some little children for their scrapbooks. In running through the pictures to find the ones I liked best, I found the envelope containing the old manuscript. This was in 1921.

I read it aloud, then, to Pearl May, and I was very glad that I had written it down in 1899, because it would have been impossible for me to do it at any subsequent time. The boys were very much pleased with it and urged me to begin where I had left off and write all I could remember. And so because they wanted me to and because I thought they might consider it an interesting story and like to read it someday, I set at it again and filled in the story from the place I had left off in 1899. I didn't bring the story completely up to date in 1921; I only brought it up to about the time I had begun to write the story (1899). I could have written a great many things about the years that followed, but my sons can remember for themselves the greater part of that period.

My life has been a very full and busy one as well as a very happy one. I have lived more than three-quarters of a century now—the first part of my life, my childhood, was spent in Pennsylvania; the second part, my adolescence, on a pioneer farm in central Kansas; the third part, my early adult years, as a school teacher in Holton and Topeka, Kansas. Then for forty years I lived in the city of Topeka, and now for nearly twenty years I have lived at Oakwood, in the country just outside of Topeka.

What I have written in the pages to follow speaks for itself, but I wanted to explain how I came to write it. I should never have thought of putting it

in book form; that was my sons' idea. They said
they wanted printed copies for themselves and that
they were sure some other people would, too. It
was they who urged me to write a brief summary of
the days since 1900, especially the history of my
Bible Class, which has been such a great part of my
life for so many years. These portions I added in
September, 1939.

                                   Flo V. Menninger

Oakwood
Topeka, Kansas
October 1, 1939

ILLUSTRATIONS

DAYS OF MY LIFE

Chapter 1

I WAS born in the home of my grandfather, near Clear Spring, York County, Pennsylvania, on April 23, 1863, the first of eight children. It was near the close of the Civil War. Mother has often told me how I was startled from my sleep by the sound of cannon in the battle of Gettysburg. We were eighteen miles from the fighting, yet the thud and roar of the cannon were plainly heard. The noise resembled that made by heavy pieces of wood rapidly drawn along a picket fence.

Mother told me how, holding me in her arms, she stood very near to President Lincoln on the day he spoke the immortal words that all the world knows today, "—that we here highly resolve that these dead shall not have died in vain—that this nation, under God, shall have a new birth of freedom— and that government of the people, by the people, and for the people, shall not perish from the earth."

My father was drafted for the army on three different occasions. The first time he was excused, for some reason I do not know. The second time he sent a substitute. The third time he was all fitted out and ready to go the following week, but the surrender of Robert E. Lee made it unnecessary.

15

When my parents were first married, they set up housekeeping with my mother's parents, whose name was Heikes, and lived with them for five years; so it came about that I was born in the same place where my grandfather and my mother were born.

When I was two years old, father and mother left me at home while they went on a visit out west —all the way to Ohio, and that was a very long way at that time. They were gone for six months. When they came back I did not know them and could not be induced to take their advances kindly. The very first thing in my life that I remember is that this strange man and woman tried to get me to go with them; I did not want to go, but in spite of my protest they took me somewhere in the dark and I was afraid.

What they really did was to put my little bed in their room to relieve my grandmother. My father was very sure that a child should always be made to obey its elders. Mother says they coaxed and kissed and tried in every way to get me to yield willingly, but I would say, "No, no! I want my mamma" (meaning grandmother). However, I was put where they wanted me in spite of the fact that I cried myself to sleep every night. My father said I must be taught a lesson in obedience. Fortunately for me, before many weeks a baby brother—little Howard —came to mother, and father was very glad to have an excuse to turn me back to my grandmother again.

I called my mother Mamma Manda and my

My Mother and I Were Born in This House—Near Dillsburg, Pa.

father Papa Sam. For a long time I insisted that I
did not like Papa Sam, and I remember distinctly
that I was afraid of him. Mother tells me that I
spoke my first words when I was seven months old,
walked at nine months and talked as much at one
year as any of her other children did at two.

When my third birthday came, we left the old
homestead and went to Franklintown to live. It was
only three miles away and was colloquially known
as "Buttstown." I cannot remember much about
our life there except that just across the street from
us there was a haunted house, in which the doors
would not stay closed and where people were afraid
to live. I never saw the ghost that was supposed to
haunt it, but was quite sure there was one and we
children would talk about it in our play.

On New Year's Day, 1868, brother Dave was
born, and on the first of April we moved to Mechanicsburg, where I began to live an existence of
my own. From this point on, I remember things
very clearly.

In Mechanicsburg, we were twelve miles from
grandfather's, and often Howard and I would go
home with them to stay a while after they had been
to visit us. On one of these occasions I had a sad
experience which left a bitter memory. Howard was
a wilful baby and would do just about what he
wanted to do. I was expected to keep him out of
mischief, but often it was out of the question for
anyone to do that. We were both only babies, and

now and then I saw nothing wrong in the thing he wanted to do, so I would help along.

We were on a visit to grandfather's farm when Uncle Amos (my mother's brother) was to be married, or to celebrate his marriage which had taken place elsewhere a few days before. I cannot recall the exact facts, but there was going to be a big party. A band was to play, and the big oven had been filled more than once with pies and cakes; there were cold turkeys and other meats and cider and apples and everything nice. Hurry and bustle and commotion filled the house, especially the kitchen, and that was where we wanted to be.

I am sure we must have been a great deal of trouble around the house, for we were sent to the barn to amuse ourselves as best we could. We were told that we could come to the party with our best clothes on if we were good, but if we bothered grandmother or the others, we would have to go to bed.

We tried to be good, for we did want to see everything that was going to happen. I can see us now, climbing on the haymows, sitting in the wheat bins and playing, as children play in the sand pile, turning the fanning mill, climbing over the threshing machine—from one thing to another, glad for every new thing. But time passed slowly; we wondered what they were doing at the house; we wanted something to eat and, even more, something to do to make the time seem shorter.

In this most trying situation, Howard had an

idea. "We will hunt the eggs and save grandmother's time, for she will be so busy tonight," he
said. This seemed a most kind and delightful thing
to do, so I heartily agreed. We found a basket and
went to work. We had often followed grandmother
on her rounds among the chickens, and we knew
pretty well where to look for eggs. We found a
goodly number of setting hens, but did not know
that we must not meddle with these. We drove
every one of them from the nests within our reach,
either mildly or by force, and picked up every egg
we could find. Oh, how happy we were, for we soon
had more eggs than we had ever seen gathered before. It took both of us to carry the basket from
nest to nest.

There was only one more place to look, and to
reach it we had to climb up on a box; even then the
nest was overhead. We did not know that the night
before grandmother had removed an old mother hen
from that very spot and left some bad eggs in the
empty nest.

Howard reached into the nest and felt two eggs.
He tried to grasp both of them, but his little hand
could only hold one well. Just at that moment we
heard someone coming. It startled us both—and
down came the eggs, breaking all over him and me,
too, for I was holding the box and reaching up to
take the eggs.

It was an awful moment, but the worst of it was
that there was grandmother and, in her German
language which we very well understood but did

not speak, she was saying that we had to be shut in the hen house and could not be washed off until bedtime. That was a terrible sentence. But just then she spied our basket of eggs and in a moment understood what we had done. She was so very angry that she forgot what she had said a moment before. She took one of us on either side of her and started for the house, but once outside the door of the hen house, she let go our hands and hurried us on with, "Get along to the woodshed and I'll be there."

Poor little Howard's eyes were blinded by the rotten eggs, and in our hurry he stumbled and fell face down on the stone walk. He did not get up nor move nor cry. Grandmother picked him up and carried him into the house where soon half a dozen women seemed to be washing his face at the same time. When he came to, I was punished. It was all my fault, they said. I should have taken care of him because I was the oldest and knew better.

That night Howard sat in his high chair, his head all tied up, seeing all the company and having a good time. I was shut upstairs alone, without one bite of the party fare. I could hear the band play, but that only added to my bitterness, for I knew all the men were in uniform—red coats with gold stripes, blue pants with white stripes, and caps to match. And there was a big drum and a little drum and golden horns that made the music. I thought it would be *such* a beautiful sight.

Dear old grandmother did what she thought was right and best for me, but that was one of the blackest days of my life and one I never deserved. I did not know that we were doing anything wrong; we were just trying to help in the only way we knew.

Brother Elmer was born in December, 1869, and I was early initiated into the task of taking care of the baby—in fact, the whole family of babies, but I liked them and did not mind at all. Elmer was a weak, sickly baby from the first and, as I think of it now, it seems to me there was always something the matter with him while he was little; he was three years old before he could run about and play with the rest of the children.

Papa was anxious that I should be a good scholar and began to teach me when I was very young. I do not know when I learned to read. I would study my lessons while I rocked the cradle, and when papa came home at night he would hear me recite them.

I started school at the age of six and was put in the third grade because I knew the multiplication tables and all the other required work except writing. This the teacher thought I could make up with the aid my father would give me at home.

I was too small to sit in the schoolroom seats, so the teacher put me on the wood box because it was a little lower than any of the seats. The hinges on the box had been broken, however, and perhaps the lid had not been laid on very carefully. At any rate, as I squirmed about, it went down and I fell into the box, my feet and head both in the air together. I was taken out quite unhurt but greatly humiliated.

I did not want to go back to school, but there was nothing else to be done. I had to go.

It was a great ambition of my father's that I should never be absent a day from school, but he did not live to see how well I succeeded.

That first year in school was hard for me and it was chiefly the task of learning to write that made it so. There seems to be no easy, short way to learn writing.

I did not finish my second year, for we moved to the country in the early spring. One day during the winter, I begged to be allowed to take Howard to school with me. He was only four years old. Mamma put a hood on him, and we started off together, feeling very big. We had not gone far when we met some little boys about my own age who were in the first grade. They disliked me because I was ahead of them in school, and they began to tease me about my baby and his hood. Howard was a little fighter, and in a minute his hood was in the snow and he said he would not put it on again. He began snowballing the boys with all his might. He soon was a sight, and I did not know what to do with him. He shouted that he would kill the boys, and they enjoyed his spunk until the school bell rang. Then Howard went home without his hood and mittens, and I asked the teacher if I could be excused so I might go home and tell mamma what had happened. I never tried taking him with me again.

Although he was such a little boy, Howard was

constantly doing naughty things; he would steal and tell stories and play tricks of all sorts. Repeated punishment of the ordinary kinds seemed to do no good. One day he took mother's pocketbook, containing all papa's earnings for the month, from the bureau drawer and went downtown with it to buy candy. The man in the store knew him, so he took the money and sent a note back to mother in the empty pocketbook telling her he had it.

Another time he took mother's purse—the kind that unfolds so that the bills lie perfectly flat—out on the front doorstep. Here he opened it, took out one bill and trudged off downtown with it, leaving the open purse on the step. In a few minutes a man came along and saw the money lying there, all ready to fly away with the first breath of wind or to be picked up by any passer-by. He must have been a really honest man for he rang the doorbell and pointed out the purse to mother. She was greatly surprised, as you might know, and thanked the man most heartily. There were fifty dollars in the pocketbook, and it would have been a great loss.

In spite of his mischief, I used to think Howard was the most wonderful boy in the world. He could do so many things and do them so quickly. He had so much energy that, when nobody had time to tell him stories or keep him busy in some way, he just had to do things of his own planning. I did wish he would not choose to do a lot of the things that he did do but, even so, I thought he was the handsomest and smartest little boy anywhere.

In our kitchen there was a fireplace with doors, in which mother kept some kindling and her dough tray, using it as a sort of closet or pantry. But Howard knew that people built fires in fireplaces for he had seen them do so. One day he found a match; the chimney corner was open, revealing a nice little pile of shavings, so you will not be at all surprised when I tell you that he lit the match and held it to the shavings. Pretty soon he had a good big fire, and by the time mother arrived on the scene, her dough tray was all ablaze and there was danger of the house catching fire. The dough tray was a long, narrow, wooden box with a lid; mother kept her flour in one end and, on baking day, mixed her bread in the other. It was painted pea green and mother thought it was very nice. She brought it with her to Kansas, and it stood in her pantry for years bearing mute testimony to Howard's mischief.

He also shaved the corners of the furniture with a butcher knife and cut the edges and fringes from everything he could reach. Once he ran away and was lost, and he was not found until late at night. He loved to tease me and other children and to take things away from us just to hear us yell and see us run. He was never so happy as when he was in a fuss with someone. He dearly loved to fight—or do anything that kept up a commotion. When he was awake, he was always up to some sort of mischief.

He grew worse and worse until just before one Christmas, the climax came. No punishment seemed to avail; no Santa Claus promises led to better ways.

Finally, one day, papa and mamma said they were going to sell him to the dogman. The dogman was a character of the town. He bought and sold dogs, and every so often he would make the rounds of the town leading a large group of dogs. We knew him well because he fed his dogs at the back of a butcher shop plainly visible from our home.

We were both afraid of him, and shuddered to think it was to this horrible character that Howard was to be sold if he persisted in being naughty. One week he was worse than ever before. Papa came home early one Friday evening with word that the dogman was coming for Howard. The dogman had said he could use Howard to help take care of the dogs. Mother picked up a little bundle of Howard's clothing, and father took Howard's hand and started across the street to meet the dogman. You should have heard his screams—and mine were wilder than Howard's. I begged them not to send him away, but papa relentlessly took him by the hand and went straight over to the dogman. The three talked a long time, it seemed to me. Finally papa came back, and the dogman went down the street with Howard and his little bundle. I wanted to ask about Howard and coax for him, but I knew better. Papa and mamma had nothing to say to each other, but both seemed very much occupied with something or other all the time.

When the table was set for supper, there was no plate for Howard. It was awful. And how I did wish mamma would not put on a plate for me. I knew I could not eat without Howard. I sat by the window crying and wondering what he would do when it was dark and time to go to bed. Visions of him sleeping with all those dogs and that dreadful man were most terrifying. I saw the windows light up here and there, and the lamp lighter climb his little ladder and light his lamps. And then I saw a little boy right under the light—another look told me it was Howard! I was out and off and by his side in a moment. Hand in hand we came marching home to papa and mamma, with copious tears and great promises. A plate was set on the table and the troubled family reunited. I do not know how long the good spell lasted, but I do remember that the mere mention of the dogman was enough to turn both our faces white for a long time afterward.

Another incident happened in this little town that you would enjoy. Baby Elmer was about all that mother could take care of, and Dave was not well either, so a woman was hired to help with the work. Howard and I were thrown upon her mercy. She proved lazy and shiftless, and did not give us enough to eat. One day Howard stole everything edible from the house and hid it in the backyard. Then he helped me to climb on top of the coal shed, handed me his loot and climbed up himself. There we sat and ate all we wanted. The funny part of it was that the woman was too dignified to climb up on the roof as we had done, so she just stood there and watched us eat. She ordered us down, but we did not come until we were ready. Howard always thought that a very clever trick and told it with great gusto to the family after the maid had departed.

To help make the winter more interesting, an epidemic of measles came to town, and our family promptly responded. All four children took the disease at the same time. The two youngest were very ill. Howard and I were put in a room together and the windows were darkened. We did not like it at all and insisted on getting out of bed and going to mother and the other children. When father came home and mother told him how we had been acting, he nailed a big board to either side of the bed, and the covers were fastened to the four corners. We stayed there until he said we might be helped over the top and to the floor.

A thrilling event happened on Halloween and it was not at a party, either. Just as children do now, everybody tried to frighten everybody else. We were out on the walk in front of our house when a boy came along wearing a false face. We had never seen one before and we tried to run, but instead, pushing and bumping against each other, we knocked Dave down on the curbstone, and Howard and I both fell on top of him. His ear struck the sharp stone and was cut quite in two. Mamma said we were careless and thought she would teach us a lesson by letting us see the doctor put several stitches into the ear to pull it together. I have never felt this was a wise thing to do.

Another occurrence is impressed deeply on my mind and has made me careful through the years.

We used the common Pennsylvania hard coal for heating and one night when we went to bed the stove had not been properly closed. The gas that escaped during the night made the entire family ill. We were living in a double house and at ten o'clock in the morning the neighbors became uneasy because it was so quiet on our side. They pounded on the wall and then rapped on the door. Getting no response, they finally broke in through the window to see what was the matter. They found every one of us unconscious, and it was only after long, hard work that we were all pulled through; some of us were sick for some time.

It was while we lived in Mechanicsburg that I learned to sew. On my fifth birthday, I had finished all but three patches for a quilt and papa was so anxious that I should get it all done on that day that he said he would make one for me if I would make two; this we did and the quilt was completed. By my tenth birthday, I had made twelve quilts, but I have never made another since, and think now that I never will.

It was the strong belief of my mother and my grandmother that every girl ought to have a lot of quilts and bedding made up so that when she wanted to go to housekeeping, she would have something to start with. They told me often of the many things they made when they were girls and recounted the contents of their wonderful hope boxes. They thought to have me profit by their example, but when I was married, I didn't have one thing that counted.

I did fritter away some money, a lot of time, and more eyesight than I had any right to use on making a fine suit of underwear trimmed in pink chambray and darned net. I had it nicely folded away to be brought out on my wedding day, but when that day came, our decision to be married was made so suddenly, I never once thought of it and for years afterward it remained in my mother's bureau drawer in the country. I was married in Holton, Kansas, in coarse cotton underwear and, on our wedding night, slept in a tennis flannel nightgown.

I never missed all the sheets and pillowcases and the dozen suits of underwear that I had been told every thrifty girl provided for herself before she would think of getting married. I thought nothing whatever about it at the time, and my judgment at present is that too much time is spent thinking about getting married—and about what to wear. I am not sure that I have done the right thing on every occasion through the years, but I am very certain as far as my marriage is concerned, that it was just the thing for us to do and that we did it in just the right way.

When I was six years old I had a beau. We went to school hand in hand and, being neighbors, we played together a great deal. His name was Willie Barracks. I did not see him after leaving Mechanicsburg until I was fourteen. Then he came out on an excursion to spend a day on the Camp Grounds.

He was sixteen. We met and spoke but had lost all interest in each other.

I do not know why papa and mamma decided to move away from the town and I have often thought about it. But the more I think about it, the more I realize that the wonder is not so much that they moved away as that they ever went there in the first place. They were both born in the country and naturally belonged there. Perhaps in town there was more to be done in papa's line of work—carpentry. At any rate, while I was still six, they bought a little farm in Adams County, and early in the spring we moved.

It was a queer little isolated spot, reached only through lanes. It seems to me now that more things happened in that secluded spot than in any other—that is, things that counted in my life.

Father went on with his carpentry work, leaving home on Monday morning and returning on Saturday night. Usually he left so early and returned so late that we children were in bed, so during the summer we saw him only on the Sabbath Day. We went to Sunday school, where papa was the Superintendent, and mother always attended, too, though how she did it I don't know.

In the winter, papa taught school for four or five months, but he was always near enough to be at home with us at night.

Chapter 2

WAS there anything my mother didn't do? I think she had a body of iron and a will of steel. We had scarcely settled on the little farm before it began to teem with life. Mother soon had a cow, pigs, chickens and ducks. In a few weeks the garden was planted, and in a few more weeks it was green with growing things. Baby chickens shared the yard with the children and it was hard to say which grew faster.

Just as soon as the sun began to peep over the hills, my mother was out in the garden hoeing, and she kept at it until the babies waked and she had to come in and attend to them. Then she would see to our dressing and get our breakfast. After milking the cows and feeding the chickens, she would be off to the garden again, with "Now, Flolly dear, you wash up the dishes like a good little girl, and take good care of the baby."

If she grew too tired or finished before it was time to prepare the dinner, she would pick up her sewing, which was always close at hand. Sitting near me, she would direct my work for I was taught early how to do this "nice stitch," how to "turn that seam," how to do this or that for the baby, how to cook some dish or other. And all this time she herself did a score of things.

The garden was very close to the house, so when baby slept it was great fun to be out with mother hoeing in my own little spot of garden with a crooked stick. One day, when I was playing that I was sticking radish seeds around the edge of the bed, something happened. Howard and Dave were outside the garden fence throwing stones. Mother told them to stop it, but they wanted me to come out and play with them and because I would not go Howard said he would hit me with a stone. Little stones kept falling all about me, but I was not at all frightened and stood up straight to tell him so. Just at that moment, a stone struck me over the left eye. I did not remember anything more until the doctor had come and put several stitches through the wound. I heard him say to mother, "A very fortunate accident—a little bit lower would have cost an eye and a little higher, a life." And then, to Howard, "Little man, I would never throw stones at my sister or anyone else again." A long white scar and a marred eyebrow tell the story of that adventure.

Our house was old and not very large. The kitchen had once been a log shanty and the other parts of the house had simply been built onto it. At one end of the kitchen was the kind of old-fashioned fireplace that one often reads about but rarely sees nowadays. The bake oven was built up against the house and the chimney and had a very peculiar hunched appearance. I remember seeing mother nail pieces of tin over holes in the kitchen floor so the children could not get their feet through them. From the kitchen, one entered a broad hall from which a long straight staircase led to one big room overhead. I always imagined those stairs were infested with rats, for I had read a story somewhere of just such stairs where rats were ever at play, and I was never comfortable in that hall alone.

Downstairs and across the hall from the kitchen was another large room, but papa put in a partition and in the winter it made a handy room in which to keep the smaller children. Over the kitchen was a loft, reached only from the upper hall by means of a hole cut through the logs.

There were no windows in the loft and all the light that entered came in through chinks between the logs. It was a scary hole, but there we kept our nuts in the winter and were sent to bring them down, in the dark as well as in the light.

Sometimes a flying squirrel, a rat or a mouse— once a nest of bumblebees—helped to make it doubly interesting and frightful to us. I saw plenty of real ghosts in that loft, and some of them will stay in my memory as long as I live.

Around three sides of the house, some fifteen feet away, was a picket fence. On the fourth side was the garden and this too was enclosed by a fence. It was my work each spring to whitewash those fences. It took me a long time to do it, and I think in the end mother did most of it.

The barn was a very old-fashioned one with a

thatched roof. There was a big floor, with a hay-mow on either side, where we children had lots of jolly good times. I had read "Darius Green and His Flying Machine" and had a vague, fanciful idea that it was in just such a place that he worked out his wonderful invention. We fixed up more than one contraption, mounted as high as we could and then, in imitation of the great Darius, let ourselves fly down on to the hay, risking our necks and a good many other things.

There was the usual barnyard with pigpen and corncrib near by. Back of the barn was a fine little apple orchard, and although it had only a few trees, there was a good variety and plenty of fruit for our use.

There were six very small fields, as I recall, and each was interesting for some special thing. In one there were several clumps of chestnut trees that bore plentifully every year. In the meadow near the house was a big shellbark hickory tree, which yielded bushels annually.

I did not know much about fairy stories, but I peopled the branches of this old tree, or the spot beneath them, from all the stories that I knew. I named the tree Goliath and when my father asked me one evening why I had done so, I said "Because he takes care of us all the week while you are away." He said, "God takes care of you——not Goliath." I answered him by saying, "God is watching Goliath, and if he does not do the right thing, God will send a stone of fire right out of David's sling,

that he has saved up in heaven, and he will kill
Goliath." Father said, "That is a funny story for a
little girl to think about a tree." But I believed it.

That was a dear meadow where Goliath stood.
From the time the dandelions began to bloom in the
spring until it was covered with snow in the fall, it
was full of wonderful things. Some distance from
the house was a never-failing spring. In the drain of
it, papa fixed a long wooden box in such a manner
that it was always full of clear, cold running water,
and in that box mother kept her milk and butter and
anything else she wanted to keep cool in the warm
weather. There was a big tree growing right over
the drain, and under this tree, grew great bunches of
honeysuckle, or, more correctly, arbutus.

The drain from this spring furnished great entertainment. It swarmed with frogs, and when the
night came down they would sing and sing! We
liked to catch them and play with them. Papa said
he would like to eat them, so we often caught a
bucket full with which to greet him on Saturday
night, but none of them was ever killed or harmed in
anyway. Sometimes we would tie strings to their
legs, carry them some distance from the spring and
then watch to see how long it took them to go back
again.

In the meadow was a bed of wild strawberries
and another of delicious black dewberries. Near the
fences, here and there, were plenty of raspberries and
blackberries. On top of a hill near one of the lanes
leading to the main road were a number of black

cherry trees from which we gathered all we could use; and last but not least there were several persimmon trees, the fruit of which kept our mouths puckered from the time they began to turn yellow until Thanksgiving time.

A family with growing children could scarcely ask for anything more ideal. There we were out in the country all alone, with everything we needed to eat and with fine opportunities of knowing nature at first hand. We were very happy together. Our parents thought we were fine children and that they were doing just the right thing for us. In a little while, they thought, we would all have homes of our own.

I remember how lovingly father and mother used to walk to the spring together on a Sabbath evening arm in arm. We children would play about them, and they would talk of the things we would have and do someday. How mother did work all that first summer! In spite of the fact that Charley was due to be born in August, mother took garden truck, chickens and seasonable fruits to market in Papertown, ten miles away across the mountains. She went until two weeks before the baby was born.

She kept on going to market for the next three years, sometimes twice in one week, and she raised, gathered and prepared everything she took to sell. Howard or Dave usually went with her, while I was left at home with the babies.

She would get up very early in the morning, feed the horse (which had been borrowed from grandfather), milk the cow and get breakfast, leaving ours on the table for us to eat when we awoke. Then she would hitch up her horse and go. She seldom came home before nightfall and we children would be in bed, having left the milking for her to do. Sometimes, the second year, I would try to do it for her, but I did it poorly; and then too sometimes, childlike, I did not feel like doing it and didn't.

Mother never complained that anything was too hard for her; she sang as she went about her work and urged us on in our little tasks. Everything she did and everything we did was done for papa to see when he came home from his work Saturday night. We worked for papa and were *good* for papa and we *lived* for papa. As I think of those days now I know my mother was constantly thinking of, working for and dreaming of her lover husband, for I am sure they were devoted lovers.

I can see mother now, on a Sunday morning, showing papa the money she earned through the week; he would put his arm about her and tell her she was a brave woman and had earned almost as much as he had, and I think it was often true.

Poor mother! I did not understand how hard she was working and what a difficult time she was really having. It seemed to me I had the worst of it. It was so hard to stay alone all day, and often the children would be so bad and the baby so cross; and mamma would scold me now and then because I was not more careful.

It must have been dreadful for her to go away and

leave her little children at home alone. I have heard her say that she cried a great many times when she left us and wondered if all would be well when she came back again, and that she was glad to see the house standing when she came back at night. It was because God was good, she said, and she never forgot to pray that we would be protected and brought through the days safely.

No doubt her prayers were answered for we never had an accident that did more than break some of the furniture or china. Once we accidentally drowned some cats and chickens; another time we moved everything we could carry from the kitchen out into the backyard. We were playing gypsies and were camped under a cherry tree. Another time I tried to whip Howard because he insisted on grinding corn through the coffee mill, and he beat me and the baby so badly that we were sore for days.

It is only fair to Howard to tell you his purpose in using the coffee mill to grind corn. The corn had to be shelled for the chickens, and mother said it was better to have it shelled for the pigs, too; moreover, the cobs were nice and clean then for use in the cookstove. So one job that we children had to do, and one that never would be finished, was to shell corn. It grew hard and monotonous, but we had it to do. We also shelled corn to take to the mill to be ground into meal for mush. We ate this with milk at night —and we always made sure there was enough left over to fry for breakfast. Howard conceived the idea of crushing the corn into meal in the coffee grinder so that mother would not have to spend time going to the mill, and I think that was very clever for such a little boy. I am sorry now that I tried to punish him.

During the third summer on the farm, we had an experience that was rather exciting. There were bumblebees and wasps and hornets aplenty, and they built their nests in all sorts of places. Howard early learned to handle the bumblebees, and he knew that wasp stings hurt more than those of bees. So he seldom molested them. But he did *not* know about hornets.

Early in the summer, some hornets began to build a nest from the lower limb of a large tree just back of the barn. Mother tried to break it up, but the hornets won out; they worked all summer long until finally they had a nest quite as large as a big bucket, cone-shaped with the point downward. It hung too high to be reached by any pole we had, but Howard was itching to knock down that hornets' nest. Mother had warned him to keep away from it, saying the hornets would not molest him if he left them alone, but Howard never gave up an idea once he fastened on it, and he meant to get that hornets' nest. So one day when mother had gone to market and taken Dave with her, Howard gathered together some stones and began a raid on the nest. The hornets became very angry. Finally he broke the nest from the limb and it fell to the ground—but mercy me! Those hornets went after him in good shape and followed him everywhere. They did not stop

with Howard. They stung the little calf in the barnyard until it bellowed. The dog yowled and the cat
crept under the corncrib. Howard came running to
the house with the angry hornets after him, and
both Elmer and I were stung by them. When mother
came home it was dark, but that did not protect her
from being stung too. Howard concluded that nothing could run away from an angry hornet.

In August of our first year at the farm, mother
waked me one night and told me she was so sick she
was afraid she was going to die. She begged me to go
for Mrs. Bushy, a neighbor who lived about a quarter of a mile away. But I was afraid of the dark and
would not go, so she went herself. I could hear her
moaning as she put on her clothes, but soon I was
fast asleep. One sleeps and forgets easily at seven.
Next morning it was Mrs. Bushy who called me
to get up and fix the breakfast for, she said, mamma
was sick and had a new baby in bed with her.
Mother has told me since how she suffered that
night, and that she and Mrs. Bushy had not been in
the house ten minutes before the baby (Charles)
was born. I accepted the baby and loved him, but in
just a month he went away from us without any
apparent cause. I wonder now how he stayed so
long, when I think of the struggle my mother had
before he came.
That was my first experience with death, and I
could not understand it. Why did they cry about the
baby, and why did they say, "He is dead"? To me,

he seemed only to be asleep. They dressed him in the best baby clothes we had. Why they should do that and then bury him in the ground was a sore problem to me. I cried about the little dress, for once it had been mine. I think mamma never had time to make anything pretty for her babies after Howard came. Her life was always filled with stern necessity that demanded essentials and not extras.

I made so much ado about the baby clothes that were gone that mamma finally threatened to whip me if I mentioned them again, and she said, "Baby went to heaven to be a little angel, and he would feel sad to be there without any clothes on. Surely you would want our baby to look as nice as the other babies in heaven." I suggested to her that all the angel pictures I had ever seen had no clothes on at all, and most of them had only heads and wings. She did not punish me for this retort but I saw her cry, and I do not believe I ever brought up the matter again. I did not stop thinking about it, however, and I am quite sure that I learned a hard lesson all by myself. I would not willingly expose a child to the mystery of death. I did not want my boys to see a dead person until they were old enough halfway to understand the answers to their questions.

Our second year in the country brought little change. We children grew and had a good time. Papa kept on with his work and mamma kept on raising chickens and vegetables and going to market. We were only three miles from mother's old home, and Howard and I would often walk over and stay all night. It took us a good while usually, for we would loiter and play along the way.

About halfway there, we had to go past a rather dense but pretty bit of woodland. We could go around it by following the road, or we could cut off a half mile or more by walking directly through it. To go by way of the road was the most fun because there were all kinds of nuts to be found—acorns, walnuts, beech, hazel and "chinkapence" (chinquapins)—besides sassafras and slippery elm. Always something to gather that we liked.

But these same big old trees furnished good places for campers and they were often used by them. It was a famous place for the gypsies, and one day when we came by, there were a lot of them there. We had never seen so many at one time before. They stopped us and talked to us and asked us a lot of questions about ourselves and our family—how far we had come and how much further we had to go and other things. When we told the folks at home about it they said it was a mistake to tell people we did not know about our affairs, and we were told never to stop and talk to anyone by the wayside again. I am not sure how well we kept that promise, but at least we did get the idea that gypsies should be avoided, for sometimes they took little children along with them, especially if they were very beautiful. Howard explained our safety by saying, "Flory isn't beautiful enough for them to take along, and they're afraid of me," and perhaps that is why we were always safe.

This little strip of woodland was known as a peat bog, because it was a low, wet piece of ground on which a great many logs lay rotting. At night, many spots on the bark looked as if they were on fire. Lots of stories were told about this spooky place, wonderful tales of how, especially on Halloween, ghosts held orgies in these woods and the will-o'-the-wisps (for that was what the lights really were) drove them about like mad. I have seen the lights many a time but not on Halloween. I used to ask to be taken there on that special night but I never was. I am afraid too good a children's story would have been spoiled had they done so.

In the daytime, the trees were full of birds. The one that attracted us especially was the woodpecker with his bright red head, and to Howard and me it seemed sometimes that his thud, thud, thud, had something to do with the ghosts that we were sure were hiding there to come out when the night was dark, and bad little boys and girls and men and women, too, came that way.

We met other hindrances sometimes on the way to grandfather's house. One beautiful day in summer we started right after dinner, our noonday meal, to go to grandfather's for the night and return the next afternoon. We started in good glee, anxious to cover the ground and get there. Howard said we could save time by cutting through Burkholder's pasture. Near the middle of the pasture stood an apple tree, as we well knew, and I rather think that was the true reason for our plan to save time, though we had plenty of apples at home. We both knew perfectly well that these neighbors had a billygoat, and we had heard that sometimes he would run at children and give them a butting, but this did not occur to us when we started across the pasture. We reached the tree, which Howard climbed promptly. He looked around—and there was billy, making for the apple tree. Howard dropped down hurriedly and helped me up, and he followed just soon enough to keep from billy's horns. But billy was not going to let us get away without punishment; he would not let us get down but stayed right there until the boy came for the cows and sheep in the evening. We turned and went home to mother, very penitent, and promised anew not to play by the way when we were going anywhere.

In August of this year, 1872, another baby came to our home—Harry—and again mother was alone. This time, however, she had arranged to signal Mrs. Bushy by blowing the dinner horn, so she was soon on hand, and there was no risk to mother. We were all glad to see and have the little one and enjoyed him for six weeks. But then he, too, went away. Mamma had worked as hard as ever before he came. She had no milk of her own for him, and he just seemed to pine away.

I was not much troubled about the way they dressed him for burial, but I began to question God's way of doing things. I understood that it cost money to pay a girl while mother had to stay in bed

—though this was not more than a week or two at the very longest, I believe. Then it took more money to buy a little box to bury the baby in, and a man had to be paid to dig a hole to put the box in, and mamma said the preacher should have some pay, too; and why in the name of wonder a good God sent babies to poor people and then took them right away when it all cost so much and they had such a hard time to get money enough to live on was a hard problem for me to solve. I thought much about it and asked just as many questions as I dared.

My dear mother made the mistake that many mothers have made. She put me off with evasions and sometimes stories. I hated such a God. Why shouldn't I? I wished I did not have to say my prayers to Him, and I could not see why He could not die and let us have a new God just as, in countries where there were kings, the people had a new king when the old one died. Maybe then we would get a better God, one who would manage to be kinder.

Remembering my own difficulties, I tried very hard to meet and answer all the questions my children asked me, in turn, and they were stunners sometimes. Their father was just as conscientious. We never put them off with any sort of excuse, although many times we could not possibly know the answer. The thing I hope I may sometime know from them is whether in their childhood they too groped and puzzled and worried as I did. I could not get anyone to tell me the things I wanted to know. My supreme effort for my own children has been to try to give them what I did not have. Maybe I will never know if I succeeded, but they themselves can decide when they read this, and perhaps do better for the little ones that may come to enrich their lives and bless their homes.

Things were really prospering beautifully about this time, and papa and mamma were very happy and contented; they were looking forward to years of joy and satisfaction with their children. The things they had planned to do were working out nicely, and the children were all well and growing, so there seemed no need for anything but thanksgiving. Hundreds of years ago Isaiah was trying to teach his people how to live and among the many wonderful messages from the Lord which he gave them, one fits this place very well—"But my thoughts are not your thoughts, neither are your ways my ways."

On a Sabbath morning in May, 1872, papa was getting ready to go to Sunday school. He had finished shaving and, looking at his face in the looking glass, he said, "Manda, I am going to take this thing off." He was referring to a queer-looking little mole that had been over his left eye, as far as he remembered, always. With those words, he took the end of his razor and cut the offending spot away. It bled so profusely and so long that he was not able to go to Sabbath school. After that it began to grow and pained him continually. In a few weeks, it had become quite a large lump. The doctor he consulted pronounced it cancer and advised him to have it burned away with caustic. Obeying orders, he went to a specialist in Gettysburg and had it done. Soon it was as large as before. The burning process was repeated three times during that year with the same result each time.

Then it was decided that the lump ought to be cut out, and father went all alone to a hospital in Carlisle, where he stayed for three months. None of the home folks could be with him. When he came back, pale and thin and with his head all bound up in white rags, we children could not recognize our papa. When the bandages were removed, and we saw the long scar and the shaved head, we were quite awed and could not understand.

The wound healed and no more lumps appeared in that immediate place, but his general health failed and he grew most miserable and suffered a great deal of pain in various parts of his body.

The long winter turned to spring, but through the days father grew weaker. The long, hot summer found him dragging himself from a chair to bed and back again. When October came, it was decided that he must keep to his bed entirely.

The noise of the children distressed him greatly and, with all her other duties, mother could not take care of him, too, though he wanted her to stay with him all the time. After some consultation, it was decided to take him to grandfather's, where he could at least have the quiet he needed and perhaps have a better chance to get well again. The move was made in November.

On the first of September, brother Noble was born and in spite of the fact that mother was so distressed over papa, he was a fine big fellow. He had to be fed on cow's milk, which was most fortunate under the circumstances. Now when mother had to go down to grandfather's to be with papa, she hired a maiden lady named Ellen Snyder to come and care for the children. Ellen's full name was Eleanora Flora Dora Albertina Liza Jane Snyder, and we called her Ellen. In later years, when I learned Lafayette's full name, I thought he and Ellen should have been married, their names were so much of a kind.

She was a great soul in spite of her names and agreed to feed four children and cuddle an infant for the sum of fifty cents a week and two lessons daily, one in reading and one in writing. She did not know one letter of the alphabet, nor could she write at all. I did the teaching—and what trials we both had! Sometimes they were tragic. I taught her in the only way I knew and the best I could, but she never ceased to complain because she did not progress more rapidly and, of course, it was all my fault. I think she made me cry every day with her scoldings.

As I think of it now, I realize that she made marvelous progress, considering that she was past forty years old. I taught her for just six months, and we read through a first, second and third reader, and

she learned to write her name. Without any inter-
ruptions or worries, that would have been great
progress. In the face of all that she had to do and the
serious trouble that worried all the household, I
think it was miraculous.

The little country school was not far away. Papa
had taught the school the two preceding winters and
we had been with him. Now Howard and I went
alone every day for five months. That was a long,
dreary winter. Mother would not come home for a
week, sometimes, and when she did come home, it
was only to go back again very soon. Ellen would
be cross to us and we did want Mother, but she only
said we must be good and do what Ellen told us to
do, for she could not come to us.

With March came the promise of spring. At last
the doctors said there was no more hope for papa;
he would soon die. He asked to be brought back to
the home where he had hoped to live with his family for such a long time, and early in April he was
made as comfortable as possible on a stretcher and
carried home. It was only six weeks until he left us
never to come back.

How fearfully he suffered through all the months
only mother knew. She was with him all the time,
through the days and through the nights. He had
nine lumps on various parts of his body when he
died. His teeth had all dropped out one by one. He
was fed for weeks through long rubber tubes, but
mother said that for a good many days near the end,
he begged to be given nothing. He deplored his con-

dition greatly on account of its effect on others. The air reeked of carbolic acid; and for a disinfectant and deodorant, sugar and coffee were thrown on red-hot coals in a long-handled pan. Those were frightful days for my father and mother.

There is an old legend that I read somewhere which says that when everything about one seems to join in a harmony of beautiful music heard at night, it was a true sign that something beloved was going away. I am quite sure that I shall never again hear anything so wonderfully sweet as my mother's voice during the long nights of the few weeks before papa died. It seemed to rest papa to have mother sing, and many times I was awakened by the lovely music. I slept just over papa's room, and I would get out of bed and creep to the stovepipe hole and listen. I was sure there were angels helping mother to sing, for I heard many voices and she was all alone. I spent many an hour during those weeks lying on the floor crying to myself while mother sang through tears in the room below.

In those last weeks father sat up just once and then his chair was pushed near the window so he could see the green fields and the cows coming down the lane. I was sitting on a stool at his feet, and mother was near by. A smile came over his face as he looked through the window, and he said, "I did not know it was so beautiful before. What a lovely waterfall, and how it trickles over the rocks. Doesn't it look nice and cool?"

"Why, Sam," mother said, "you must be dreaming."

"Oh, no, I'm not. You see it, do you not, Flolly?" he said, turning to me.

"No, papa, you must be thinking of a story," I said.

Then he said, "Oh, I see, Manda. That's on the way to heaven, and I am going, but I did not think it would be quite so soon. You will be lonely when I am gone, but you will take good care of the children and Flolly will help you. Put me to bed now."

A few days after that we all kissed him good-bye, and on May 10, 1873, he died—just two years from the time he removed the fatal mole.

My father's family, the Kniselys, had been keeping Elmer that week and when the news reached them, grandmother came and brought him with her. When they arrived, she and mother sat in the kitchen and talked, taking no notice of what Elmer was doing. Following the custom of the time, papa had been laid out on a board in the room that had been his. All at once, Elmer burst into the kitchen holding the cloth that had covered papa's face, and he said, "My papa is not dead; he's just asleep." Going into the room, they found the sheet on the floor, the bandage pulled from the chin and the coppers from the eyes. Elmer had pulled down everything he could.

Grandmother thought he ought to be punished but mother said, no. She sat down beside the body and took Elmer on her lap. She tried to explain to him that papa had gone to heaven and that this body was only the shell of what was really our papa; she showed him that the body was cold and did not breathe and could neither talk nor see. After a little he said, "I don't want to see him any more."

In answer to Elmer's troubled questions about death Ellen, the kindly soul, had said to him that when people died, they were put into a box and then into a deep hole, where they stayed until the bugs and worms ate them up. With this conception of death in his mind, he had marched straight into papa's room to see about it. I believe it would be better to tell children the dead are "only asleep, for a long, long night."

It was the custom in that part of the country, when anyone died, for all the friends and relatives, as well as beggars, tramps and whomsoever would, to attend a funeral and to be invited home with the family for dinner. Some even stayed for supper and a few all night. Only a pauper was laid away without this honor. Consequently, the day before a funeral was a very busy one in the home of the deceased. The more popular and well known the person, the larger would be the crowd to be cared for after the burial.

Our little old house was a sight to be seen on the Sunday after papa died. Women came from all the neighborhood, bringing with them such things as would be needed to help with the preparations that had to be made. They baked pies and cakes and bread, boiled hams and killed chickens, ground coffee and pared potatoes. The long Sabbath, which had no touch of the Sabbath in it, finally came to an end, and then, on the next day, the body must be taken away.

The house and the porches and the yard were filled with the people who came to pay their last respects. Someone read from a Bible, "For I reckon that the sufferings of this present time are not worthy to be compared with the glory that shall be revealed in us," explaining that the text had been a favorite with my father. After a brief summation of his life, a song and a prayer, we made ready to leave for the cemetery.

As soon as the procession of buggies started on its way up the hill through the lane that led to the open highway, the food preparations began; and when we got home, the good women were ready for all who came. There were tables indoors and out. The people began to eat at once and they continued to eat. Eventually those who were going began to depart—but it was evening before many of them left, with the usual expressions of sympathy. Twice as many stayed all night as we had room for. How strained and uncomfortable everyone was! It seems to me now that it was a most barbarous thing to do. I have heard that this foolish old custom still prevails, but is not as rigorously followed as in those early days.

Chapter 3

WHEN the funeral was over and everyone had gone everything seemed strange. Poor mamma cried all the time. "Affairs have to be settled up," she said, though goodness knows, there was little enough to settle. However, mother had to have a sale to sell what little there was, for that was the law. In a very few months we did not have anything in the world except a debt of $300. There we were—five children—and not a thing in the world except our wonderful mother, and she *was* wonderful. I was ten years old, Noble about nine months. What could be done with us? Dear old grandfather and grandmother said it was a pretty hard proposition, but they would take us all home with them for a while at least. Some of mother's brothers and sisters opposed the plan bitterly, and who could blame them? But we went to grandfather's to live.

Mother agreed to do the work for all the family —grandfather, grandmother, a brother, one or two hired men, herself and five children—if grandfather would feed and clothe us. This meant cooking, baking, washing, ironing, milking, making butter, besides helping with the marketing. She sandwiched in when she could the sewing that had to be done.

When we went to grandfather's, they had a woman,
a maiden lady, Sue Kuchs, who had been with them
for seventeen years. They were paying her 75 cents
a week. She was to remain for a few months, the
reason for which you will see later.

How mother got through the four years we were
there, and did the work and lived to tell the tale, is
a marvel. But she did it. Perhaps an explanation of
her own gives the truest answer, "God was good and
kept me well and gave me the strength to do it; my
children gave me the ambition to do it, and so I
worked away and did it."

What an awful trial we must have been to those
two old people and that bachelor uncle!

We had not been with them many weeks when
one night (November 10, 1873) mamma was taken
very sick. Grandmother put the baby in his cradle, in
the sitting room and told me to stay there with him
and not come out. Looking through a window, I
saw an old neighbor lady come in. I heard my mother
scream again and again. I went into the kitchen,
wanting to know what was the matter, but everybody seemed to be busy and everything was in a
commotion. I was sent back to my baby with a com-
mand to stay there. Then I heard them say, "Go for
the doctor." I saw the doctor drive to the front gate
and come in, and after a while I heard them sending
for another doctor, and I saw him come. Both doctors had come in a gig (a two-wheeled affair, with
a balanced seat in the center), and as I stared at these
two vehicles at the front gate, I heard all sorts of

sounds from that back room, but not a thing did I know or understand. Noble, the baby, went to sleep in his cradle, and I fell asleep on the floor beside him.

When I awoke it was nearly daylight. I could hear people moving quietly about the house. I crept out to the kitchen and heard the faint cry of a new baby. "Oh, grandmother, do tell me what is the matter!" I cried. I think I must have screamed the words at her as she came from the back room.

"Hush, child," she said, "Mrs. R. brought you a baby sister, but your mamma is very sick, and maybe she will not get well again. You be a good girl and take care of your little brother."

Children do not always understand things, but they certainly do sense them. Perhaps their thoughts are crude and often not worth the heeding, but the fact remains that many lives are saddened by the wrong treatment of a little child.

In that moment I was wounded beyond words. It seemed to me that my heart must have left my body. I was completely dumfounded. I went back to my baby who, by the way, weighed forty pounds; and now I think it was a sin for a child of ten years to have been expected to lift him even a single time. But he was a dear, good baby and I always loved him. We called him Fatty, and he kept the name until he was a big boy.

But to return. I went back to my baby and how we ever got through the day I do not know; but I do know that I cried nearly all day and, worse still, I *thought*. I came to conclusions, too, which have never wholly left me; some of them were right and some of them were wrong. The entire world was wrong to my way of thinking. I had been told that babies were found in hollow trees entwined with ivy, and in moss-covered caves; that God planted the seeds there from which they grew, and that only doctors and very wise women knew where to go to find them. So what people did when they wanted a baby was to send word to either of these two privileged persons—and there was your baby in the doctor's satchel or in the bundle the old woman was sure to bring with her.

I reasoned with myself thus: They had lied to me. I knew my mother had never asked anyone to bring her that baby. Somehow, then, they came when people did not ask for them. And why was my mother sick? I did not care if she did die. She surely could not love little Noble or she would never have allowed anyone to bring her another baby while he was so little and needed her so. One thing sure, *I* would not love it nor do anything for it. I would always be loyal to Noble. I hated the ugly little thing—I was sure it *was* ugly. And how I did abuse it in my own mind! I stood it as long as I could, arguing to myself, and then I burst out at my grandmother with an awful speech. The gist of it was that the old neighbor woman ought to be killed and that mother ought to die for telling me such lies and that I never would look at that baby.

Grandmother took me by the shoulders and said, "Child, you do not know what you are saying. You cannot understand what we are going through. God will punish you for talking like this, just as he did the children for saying things about Elisha. Go, now, or I will whip you." In fear and anger, I left her.

I must have nearly broken her heart, for her burden was almost too much to bear, but I wish she could have known how wretched I was, and all because they thought I was "too little to understand."

Late in the evening mother grew worse and wanted to see the children. I pouted and said I would not go, but my uncle made me. I went sullenly and would not kiss my dear mother nor would I look at the baby. Mamma cried and begged me to come to her, but I insisted that she did not care anything about me or little Noble or she would not have let Mrs. R. bring her another baby. She pleaded with me in her weakness and said I was too little to know about these things; sometime she would tell me all about it. But I was wild with rage at the injustice I thought had been done and I resented all she said. Finally I was sent away in disgrace.

For days, mother's life hung by a thread, but thanks to a kind Providence, I was spared the remorse and humiliation that would always have been mine had she died. It was some weeks before she was able to be around with us, but when she was, I had changed. I felt that I had no friends, that somehow they were all treating me in some way that was not right. I could not explain it, but I felt it. I was not a child any longer. I was moody and silent. I thoroughly hated the baby, and she was quite a big girl before I could bring myself to care for her. It seemed to me I could not really *love* anyone but Noble. I used to ask God never to make it necessary again for me to take care of any more babies. I seemed to be afraid of having them loaded on my shoulders from any quarter. I grew *so old,* the year my sister Leah was born. I felt as if all the world were mine to take care of, and indeed as I think of it even now, for years my share of burdens was plenty large enough.

Mother urged me to go out and play with my playmates or visit other girls my age, but I never cared to play after Leah came. When I did not have to take care of the children I liked to get off by myself with a book or my crochet needle, but somehow I could never be childishly happy. I was always thinking and dreaming about some mystery that I could not understand.

If someone had only talked to me intimately and won my confidence, all my life might have had a different outlook. Because I spent so little time with others I was spared much of the gossip that was as familiar among girls then as it is today. Often I heard things that sounded queer to me, but they were probably spoken in front of me without a thought that I did not know what was meant. It is strange that it could be so, and it is not right that it was so, but I was seventeen years old before I had a true idea of where a baby came from—an old maid told me during the time I was teaching my second term of school. Perhaps you can realize something of what it cost me to get this information in such a blunt way and to be laughed at and made fun of for my ignorance.

The new baby was wrapped in a red shawl after her daily bath. One morning mother discovered a red mark under her lower lip. She thought it was a bit of the shawl and tried to pick it off, but found it would not come off. As the days went by it seemed to grow larger, and quickly the alarm went out— a cancer! All the family and relations and friends and neighbors kept watching the spot and talking about it and expressing this opinion or that, until mother thought something must be done about it.

The thing decided upon was to take the baby to see "the powwow woman." This character was an old Negress who lived up in the mountains quite by herself. She had the reputation of having done wonderful things to right nature that had gone wrong. I had heard much about her and although I was afraid, I begged to go along when they took the baby to see her.

Grandmother and I went the first time. We drove all forenoon. The last part of the ride, through quiet mountain roads, was very beautiful. Finally we came to the little log house, tumbledown-looking enough to satisfy any imagination. It stood there all alone without a sign of anything about it that would help provide a living for the powwow woman. But we had been told that she was a great

woman and could cure the ugly cancer on our baby's
face, so nothing else made any difference.

When the door opened in answer to our rap, there
emerged from the blackness a figure even blacker.
I was terribly frightened and held on to grandmother's dress while she told of our errand. The old
woman said she could surely cure the little child and
invited us to come in. There were only two tiny
rooms. The one we entered was, I suppose, the
kitchen and living room in one. I shall not describe
it, first, because it was too dark to see things distinctly and, second, because you would not care to
know what was in it.

I shuddered as she led the way into the next room.
Here, however, there was a window, so the room did
not seem quite so gloomy, and we could see a bed
and a table as well as a chair or two. The powwow
woman was ragged and dirty in her dress, and she
rolled her eyes as she looked at the three of us until
I became more afraid than ever. I imagined she was
going to do something terrible, and maybe we would
never see our home again.

She took a look at the red spot and then brought
a board from the outer room, laid it on the table
and put the baby on it. Next she took a bottle and,
with a little stick, put some of the contents on the
red spot. Next she rolled up her sleeves, put her
hands together and began her incantations. . . . First
she put her hands on the baby's head, then lifted
them high and, moving them in a half circle, came
down at the feet; then back to the head and then

again to the feet; repeating the process over and over, swaying her body rhythmically and speaking all the time. Her eyes seemed to roll entirely around in their sockets. After some little time she let herself drop to the floor, limp and exhausted, and sat there very still with her head down. Finally she said, "Amen." Then she arose and asked for her pay. I do not know how much it was, but grandmother gave it to her and we started for home, with one glad heart at least. We were to come back on a certain day for another seance.

We arrived home safely, satisfied that a very proper and worthy and necessary thing had been done. I began to worry about the next trip, but when the time came grandmother took the baby and went by herself, without asking me to go.

I surely saw the "woman with a familiar spirit," not in Endor, but in the Blue Ridge mountains. Three times Leah was taken to the cabin in the hills and powwowed over. The red spot ceased growing and everybody was satisfied.

Sister Leah is still with us, but every grain of common sense in my body refused to give credit to that foolish superstition and the Negro powwow woman. Mother and I could never discuss the matter. Mother said, "There are so many things that I cannot understand that I won't say God did not use the powwow woman to help halt the growth of the mole on Leah's lip. I will only ask Him to keep it from taking her away from us." Mother truly believed that the incantations helped.

Though I regret the burden we must have been to our dear old grandparents, I am glad we were taken there to live with them. The farm had been in the possession of their family for generations; it contained ninety-seven acres, and was a very large farm indeed, for that part of the country. Grandfather was the eldest of five sons; there were no daughters. His mother was one of those thrifty women who could do everything. She educated her boys herself, so far as they had an education, and she found plenty of time to help her husband besides. She helped him wash the sheep in clear running water and afterward took her place at the shearing tables. She carded the wool and made it into rolls from which she spun the yarn and wove it into great bolts of cloth. From this she made clothing for her husband and boys and flannel for her own dresses. Some of the best among my grandmother's blankets and coverlets were made by this thrifty great-grandmother of mine.

She made her linen thread from flax raised on the farm and wove it into bolts of cloth from which were supplied all the linen needs of her household. I still have a piece of linen she made, that mother gave me a long time ago. Her looms and wheels were still in the family when I was a little girl.

Great-grandmother Heikes was quite a violinist. I often used to ask grandfather to tell how she taught her boys to play—it seemed to me such a funny story. He said that each of the boys, as well as *Mutter*, had a violin. Their lessontime came in the evening after the work was done. There was a big fireplace in the kitchen and she would put the slut in its place near the fire ready to begin.

I think this would be a good place to tell you about the lights used in those days—for they had not improved much in my youth. The slut was the kitchen light. It was made of tin or iron and shaped something like a flattened pear; it was about an inch or an inch and a half through. Sluts were made in different sizes and were filled with ordinary lard. A long cotton wick was put into the grease, and the end stuck out of the small end of the pear-shaped device. This was hung by a chain from a rod fastened in the wall for that purpose. A stiff wire was fastened by a slender chain to the lamp itself. This was used for digging up the wick and "fixing it" every five minutes or so by getting some of the grease into the burning end.

We also used tallow candles. We made literally hundreds of them every winter for other rooms in the house. The tallow came from the beeves killed at butchering time. (Not a bit of anything was wasted at our house.) We had candle moulds—just long tin frames with tubes the size of a candle. Some frames had six tubes and some had twelve. The wick was bought in large balls. This was wound round and round the mould until there was enough for each candle. Then it was cut in two. Next we would double one of the cut strands and roll the ends between our fingers until they would go through the small opening at the bottom of the mould. After the wick was coaxed through, we put a stick across the top of the mould and through the double part of the strand. Then we would catch the ends we had put through the bottom of the mould, pull them tight, tie them together, and one frame was ready for the tallow.

While we did all this the tallow would be melting on the stove, and as it was poured into the moulds all the wicks were balanced "exactly in the center." We liked to choose cold days to make our candles, for then the tallow would get stiff quickly and we could get more made. When the tallow was hard, we simply chipped the knots at the bottom, took hold of the stick at the top and pulled, and there was a bunch of long white candles ready for a big box in the cellar used expressly for them. They had to be kept away from rats, mice and cats and any other thing that might spoil them for use.

The tallow candle was used everywhere. We had just one coal-oil lamp and that was used only on special occasions and for company. We had all sorts of holders for the candles. One kind was used in the house and another, a kind of lantern, with openings in it, for outdoors. A funny one was the foot warmer. That opened like a chest and had little windows in it. The top was made of metal and covered with carpet. The candle warmed the top and, when the weather was cold, we put it into the buggy to keep our feet warm.

It was under the old lard light that grandfather and his brothers sat on three-legged stools, made of a slab of log, to take their music lessons. *Mutter* had a chair. She lined them up in a sort of military way and made them get good and ready before she would let them begin. Sometimes they had a good time but othertimes she punished them. Her way of keeping them to what she thought they ought to do was to strike them on the head with her fiddle bow. Sometimes merit was rewarded in a simple way, but most of the time the lessons were stern and severe.

The final result was pretty good. When I knew the family they were all interesting musicians, and grandfather said that when they were boys they often went long distances to play. I always loved to hear my grandfather play. He was not very successful in teaching his own children, although he made the effort. Once when he tried to teach them, he promised a violin to the one who learned to play a certain piece of music best in the shortest time. Mother won the violin. Leah often played it for my boys. But no one in our family has shown any special aptitude in music. Howard has amused the country people at their dances sometimes, but he does not pretend to play well.

Great-grandmother did not live to see her boys grow to manhood. Soon after she died, her husband married a woman younger than some of his boys. New children came and the family was broken up. All the boys except grandfather finally left the home place and after a while he took the farm from his

father, the latter moving his family to Mechanicsburg, where we will leave them in this story.

My grandfather was a sweet-tempered, easygoing,
simple man. He had a sort of David-like faith, and
he believed in doing something all the time. He was
full of ideas on which he often experimented, and
if they did not work out, he was not regretful and
never felt that he was to blame for their failure. One
day he concluded that the home place on which both
he and his father first saw the light of day, and
where seven children had been born to him, was getting too small for his growing family. He wanted to
sell it and buy more land closer to the mountain.
Grandmother and the older children remonstrated in
vain. He found a place he wanted as well as a purchaser for the old home, and he sold it.

The new place was not what he thought it was
going to be. First one thing and then another failed
to work out as he had planned, and he began to
worry and fret until his friends became fearful that
he was going to lose his mind. He longed for his old
home and could not keep away from it, so after two
years of terrible strain, he bought it back again, paying much more for it than he had received. He never
left it again. He tore down the old house and built a
new one for his wife and children to enjoy, and in it
they grew to manhood and womanhood. Grandfather died of apoplexy, two years before grandmother was taken in the same way.

Grandmother was the power behind the throne,
and what she said was usually the order of the day.

Sometimes grandfather did things on his own hook, however, and then they had conversations. Fortunately they were always really lovers, so in general things went smoothly.

How different it was with the Kniselys, my father's family! They lived only about three miles from the Heikes's, and we children were made to go and visit them every so often—for duty's sake, I suppose—and sometimes we had to stay for a day or two. They may have thought themselves a most interesting family, but for my part, I never liked any of them, and for good reasons, too, I think.

Grandfather Knisely was of English descent, and grandmother was Welsh. He was a large, well-built, good-looking man, but he was very stern and never smiled. He was never pleased with anyone or anything. His face seemed to be set in a mould from which it did not alter. He seldom spoke, but when he did, it seemed to me it was only to find fault about something. We were so much afraid of him that we did not need to be told to keep out of the way.

He was considered one of the best scholars in the country and taught school through many winters. At various times he held some of the county offices, but I do not know what they were. He was an extensive reader and had a fine library. I used to wish ever so much that I could take out some of the books and look at them, but I never did. I was even afraid to look at the backs of them for fear grandfather might see me and scold.

I used to think that grandmother was afraid of him, too; and I often felt that she would have paid more attention to us if she had dared. We seemed to be tolerated about the place much as the cat and dog were. We were given plenty to eat and were allowed to play about the place as long as we did not molest anything or annoy anyone, but if we asserted ourselves grandfather looked at us and that was enough to settle our mildest ambitions.

Then there was Aunt Belona—poor unfortunate! She had been a victim of "falling sickness" from childhood, and she had an everlasting headache. We would never get to the door without being accosted with, "Hush, Auntie has a headache."

Nobody ever seemed glad to see any other member of the family, and I never saw a caress or a kiss in that house. It was a cold, ghostly, old place to me, and I used to think there were things about that should not have been there. I did not know what, but I never ceased looking for *something*.

Grandfather prided himself on being, not a religious man, but a moral man. He believed in neither a heaven nor a hell. My father was never allowed to attend a Sabbath school when he was a boy, and when he grew to manhood and insisted that he would go, his father turned him out and told him to find a home elsewhere. Although he was only a boy, his father did not speak to him for five years, and it was a long time before he was allowed to go home and see his own mother.

Grandfather Knisely suffered for many years with

sore limbs and kept them bandaged from the ankles to far above the knees. This probably made him more of a recluse than he would have been if he had been well. He died in his faith at the age of sixty-eight, I think. He was found dead in his chair, with his feet on the woodbox and a book in his lap. Mother says he was often very kind and really did a lot of splendid things for people, but to me he was a stern, harsh, relentless, unforgiving, unlovable old man, and I wish he had not been my grandfather.

Grandmother Knisely was a tiny, dried-up, little body, who went stealing about to do what she could and what she thought was right, but she must have lived a very narrow and lonely life. She had four boys and two girls, but three of the boys died in infancy. Aunt Belona was an invalid as I have said, and Aunt Kate rebelled against the home government and went to the city when she was very young. There she married a man who was not very temperate, and whenever I heard about her, she was having a hard time about something.

My father was his mother's one comfort, and she was deprived of this on account of the displeasure he seemed to give his father. Sometimes grandfather would not speak to her for days after she had been to our home to see papa and his family. He never came to see us, not even when papa died. Grandmother did not long survive her son. She died the same year papa died, after an illness of a few weeks.

Aunt Belona's physical condition would naturally make her different from other people, and I remember how odd she was in many ways. She had a way of saving odds and ends of things, especially pieces of cloth. The garret was a storehouse for her various collections. The thing that attracted my attention one day when she took me with her to look for something, was a bandbox filled with silk pieces of every color and size. Immediately, I coveted some of them for my doll, but I knew there was no use asking for them. When we went downstairs the thought did not leave me, and later in the day I managed to steal up alone and take a piece of beautiful purple silk. I took it home with me and told mother that Aunt Belona had given it to me, but she knew that Auntie would never do so rash a thing as to part with any of her garret treasures. She made me take it back at the earliest convenient time and tell Auntie what I had done. That was the most difficult thing I ever had to do, and it brought many a stab to me from more sources than one for a long time afterward.

There was just one other time in my life when I did deliberately steal and lie. At the little country store where mother often sent us for things she wanted, they once had in the showcase a lot of taffy, fixed up in little braids. I thought they were lovely and wanted some badly, but each time I went, mother would say she could not spare the money. One day when I was sent on the usual errand, I had five cents more than I needed for my order; at once I thought of the scheme of getting the candy and not telling mother anything about it. I bought the candy and ate all I could, but I got home before it was all consumed. I gave what was left to Howard, and he told mother that I had given him some candy. She made me tell her all about it. Perhaps I needed both these occasions in my life, but it was years before I heard the last of my purple silk and my braided candy.

My father was a tall, slender man, with very black, waving hair, the bluest of eyes and a nervous temperament. Mother says he was the best man that ever lived. Maybe he was everything she says he was, but I wish I remembered him more kindly than I do. Mother says I have just forgotten and imagine a lot of things that were never true, and I think she is right, but one cannot help retaining the impressions one gets in childhood.

We children really saw too little of father to know him well, for he was away from home much of the time. And, like most children, I suppose, we took special delight in a romp or a fight just when he and mamma wanted to talk. So it seems to me that he scolded us just about every time he saw us. Howard's naughtiness often got us into trouble. It was father's custom to question us when he came home on Saturday night, and we had to tell him the good and the bad things we had done during the week. When he thought an offense committed by either Howard or me ought to be punished, he invariably punished both of us, for, he said, "Then I will be sure to get the right one." I did not deserve punishment a good many times and have always felt that his system was unjust. If a child is not punished for a thing when he does it, it seems to me it should be forgotten.

I was not always glad to see Saturday night and my father. One mode of punishment he used was to make us stand on top of a tall cupboard for a certain length of time. I was just a little too tall to stand erect under the ceiling, and lots of times my neck would ache into the next day. I have always felt it was wrong of him to do that. I daresay father had a fairly good education, for he taught school through eighteen winters, beginning to teach when he was only fourteen. (I taught my first term at fifteen.) Father was my teacher for two winters. One day a big boy caught me by the feet and threw me down into the snow. I went into the school-room and told father. He immediately brought the boy in and made us sit in the same seat all afternoon. I was only a little girl, but I was greatly humiliated and felt the punishment was unfair.

I realize now that my father was probably influenced by his father and that he came by his sternness naturally. I think he was fond of all his children, but I am sure that Elmer was his favorite. Mother says it was because Elmer was the baby for so long, and then, too, he was such a sickly little fellow that he naturally won more sympathy than was necessary for the other children.

I have often wondered what life would have meant to us through the years if mother had been taken from us and father left. Or, what would have happened if she too had gone six months later, as it was feared she would. Or where and what we would be today, if we had been permitted to remain an unbroken family. Who would venture an answer? Who would be bold enough to say he knew which would have been best? To feel that God knows best, and cares for us all and always, is one of the best lessons we can ever learn.

As it was, we went to the Heikes's, and no half dozen children ever had a nicer place to live than we had for four years. It was ideal in ever so many ways.

Chapter 4

THE house that our grandparents shared with us was a plain, two-story, almost square, brick structure with no additions save a porch at the front and back. There were four rooms and a pantry downstairs and four rooms and a hall upstairs. A big garret, the length and breadth of the house, was a source of much delight to the troop of grandchildren, who were allowed free access to its many treasures. It was the storehouse for the boiled fruit butters and extra cider and winter herbs and such things, but it never was too crowded for us to find room to play there, and this was never denied. It was great fun to be there on rainy days, and to listen to the patter on the roof while we played with reels and spinning wheels.

Around the house was a picket fence, and along its entire length was a flower bed that yielded every old-fashioned flower that has ever come to my notice. The tulip bed had forty different varieties the last year we were there. Against the house on the south side were chrysanthemums of all colors, that bloomed until the snow fell. At the front of the house climbing rose vines covered the wall and a part of the roof as well. What a mass of beauty this

was when it blossomed! I have never seen anything
in later years quite so beautiful as that wonderful
rose bush. Between the flower bed at the house and
the other one over along the fence, there was a brick
walk, often hard to see on account of the portulacas
that sprang up in the cracks and on sunny mornings
opened their pretty bright faces to the sun—to give
thanks for the beautiful sunshine, grandmother
said. In this same little yard there were grapevines,
a crab apple tree and a pear tree that bore much fruit
every year.

Close by the back porch were the bake oven and
the dryhouse, both under the same roof. Who
among all the people we know could tell what a dry
house or a dryer was? Yet they were common in
those days. A dryer was a wooden frame about four
feet long, with eight or ten narrow slats set with
spaces between, on which we dried the fruit. Around
the edge an upright slat kept the fruit from falling
off. Fruit was washed and dried, or prepared in
whatever way was necessary, and arranged in thin
layers on the dryers. The dryhouse was fitted up
with tiers of racks onto which the dryers were placed.
Some distance below these racks was a big long old
stove in which we burned wood four feet long.
When the trays were filled with fruit, a fire was built
in the stove and kept going until the fruit was well
wilted; then it was put out in the sun to finish dry-
ing. If it happened to be rainy, the fruit could be
dried entirely by stove heat, but we liked the flavor
better when it was finished in the sun. After the

fruit was thoroughly dried it was put into bags and laid away in the fruit chest upstairs. Bushels and bushels of it were put away in this manner every summer. If there was more than our family needed, it was taken to market where there was always a ready sale for it.

The bake oven was not specially interesting to me then, but when we came to Kansas and had to bake bread without one, I was very much puzzled. I had never seen bread baked in anything but a bake oven and I did not see how in the world baking could be done in a stove. At home we had a baking day, and it was a full day, too. Ten or a dozen *big* loaves of bread—fifty cent ones, I should think, as compared with our present ten cent ones—thirty to forty pies of all kinds and maybe a cake or two—every bit of this would be ready at the same time to be baked in the big oven.

The oven was piled full of wood four feet long which was left to burn into coals. When it was red hot, the oven was hot enough to do the baking. Then, with a long-handled scraper, the coals were pulled out and dropped through a hole in front of the door.

All the things to be baked were waiting on a great, heavy, plank table, always kept by the oven door to set things on. As soon as the coals were out of the oven, the food was shoved in by means of a long-handled flat shovel. The bread went first and the cakes, if any, came last, but all of it was put

in as rapidly as might be in order that as little heat
as possible should escape.

In an hour the baking was done, and the pies and
bread were drawn out with the long-handled shovel
and placed on the table to cool. Then everything
had to be carried to the cellar, where there were big
cupboards to hold it. If the weather was good, we
took it around the corner of the house; if the weather
was bad, we went through the kitchen. Week after
week we followed the same program. I often think
of the pie cupboard. To this day (1899), although
mother has a modern cookstove to bake in and
knows, too, that pies are better when they are fresh,
nevertheless she follows that custom of other days
and bakes three to six pies at once and then puts
them on the table morning, noon and night, until
they are eaten or turn sour and spoil.

The back porch was the most important spot on
the farm because it was to this place that we brought
the fruit and produce and prepared them for the
market. There was a big sink almost as long as the
porch itself; this was the counter on which all wares
were weighed, bunched, basketed or otherwise made
ready for the market wagon. It was here that, for
most of the year, we lived and moved and had our
being, and here even the smallest child had daily
tasks apportioned to him.

Oh, it was such a *beautiful* place; even as a little
girl, I appreciated its beauty and loved it! The porch
faced the foothills of a spur of the Blue Ridge Mountains, and one of the joys of my childhood was to

dream about those hills while I washed and tied
radishes and onions into bundles or fixed up the
berry baskets to look their best, for such work soon
became mechanical and did not satisfy my mind at
all. I fancied all sorts of queer things about those
hills and in my imagination filled them with meaning for myself. Few joys of later years have ever
been of truer inspiration to me than were those
fancies of my childhood. One fairy wish that I liked
to dream of was that a certain little hill might turn
into sugar, and that I might have the privilege of
eating a hole all the way through to the other side.
I liked sugar very much and we were not allowed to
have it very often.

All through the year those hills were a beautiful
sight from our back porch. In springtime they were
covered with green, and the green would soon be
swallowed up in the pink of the red-bud and the
white of the tasseled chestnut blooms and dogwood.
When these blossoms left, all was green again and
such a beautiful green—one green and yet so many
greens. All summer long it was fresh and cheerful
looking, morning, noon and night, in the sunshine
and in the rain. And when the cold nights came, the
hills changed in color; when Jack Frost kissed the
land, he did not miss the hills. Such browns and yel-
lows and orange and gold I will never see anywhere
else, I know. When winter winds played among the
leaves and coaxed them to the ground—suddenly,
sometimes, leaving only empty branches reaching

out toward the blue sky—we knew that pretty soon it would snow.

When the snow fell and covered everything that was low and dark and perhaps ugly, when only the big trees and the long branches thrust themselves out of the white blanket, it really seemed as if a new world had come into existence—a perfectly beautiful, wonderful world. I would look at it through the kitchen window and let my imagination run wild.

Santa Claus, of course, lived under the great white pile of snow, and I knew he was working away to get ready for the little children everywhere at Christmastime. There was a shed for his wonderful sleigh with its big buffalo robes and golden bells, kept free from dust and mice and any other thing that might spoil them. And there was a stable "warmer than any barn in all the world" fitted up with single stalls and bins full of oats and grain and piles of hay to feed the reindeers that lived in the mountain in the summertime but came to Santa's barn in time to be used when the Angel came out of the sky right over Santa's palace and sang, "Glory to God in the highest; on earth, peace, good will toward men."

The second chapter of Luke was taught to us, and its story fitted perfectly into my mountain fancies. One tree that stood out alone against the sky marked the spot from where, just overhead, the Angel came with his message to the Shepherds. They were kneeling in the snow below—a great bunch of berry bushes, half peeping out over the top of the snow. Not far away, a clump of trees which grew quite close together was the sure place to have the "heavens open for the Host." Many of my thoughts were associated with those lovely hills and they were very dear to me.

It was harder for me to say good-bye to the hills than to any of my living friends, and today their memory is the brightest thing I hold from the Pennsylvania years. I well remember how, on the last afternoon in the old home, I went out back of the bake oven and sat under a big old apple tree that commanded a view of the mountain and tried to recall the friends of my imagination, one by one, and to each I said good-bye out loud. Then I cried awhile to myself and said, "I want God to bless all of you because I love you. I know I shall miss you terribly; I hate so much to leave you and maybe I will never see you again."

It took only a few short weeks for me to learn how truly I *did* miss them, and many a time I have been very homesick to see my hills again. But I never have.

And the cellar! What a treasure house it was! I have seen it filled to overflowing more than once. Every winter it was *full*. I have seen four hundred bushels of apples in it, bin over bin, four deep; as many bushels of potatoes; five to six hundred quarts of fruit, all kinds, most of it in two-quart jars; gallons of sweet pickles, peaches, pears, green tomato pickles and the like, in two- and four-gallon stone jars; barrels of cider and kraut, and always a little wine. It was divided into a light and a dark cellar and things were put where they would keep best. It surely was a model cellar. I think all members of the family were better than average managers for nothing of any kind was allowed to go to waste, and everything was planned and worked out with great precision.

When the late grapes were picked from the vines, the finest bunches were set aside. The ends of their stems were waxed and the grapes went into paper sacks. These were tied shut and hung on the rafters of the roof in the garret; we counted on these grapes for Thanksgiving.

When the frost was about to take the tomato vines, they were pulled up by the roots and hung on the ceiling of the cellar; in that way we would have fresh sliced tomatoes often until Christmastime. We kept fresh pears for Thanksgiving and sometimes longer.

Just a few steps from the backdoor was the woodhouse stocked with many cords of wood. Grandfather owned ten acres of timber in the mountains, three miles away, and whenever the men could not work on the farm in the wintertime, they brought home the wood that had been cut and corded during the summer. This was piled up back of the woodhouse and when they had time, they hitched the horses to the power and with a circular saw cut the wood into stove or oven lengths. Then it was split and banked carefully in the shed until it was full to the doors. Wood for the oven was never cut shorter than four feet.

The sitting room was heated with a "Tin Plated" stove—just a long iron box standing on four legs about eighteen inches high. Shortly after we came to live with grandfather, he bought a big base-burner. It was practically a new thing in our neighborhood. This had a big magazine that led straight overhead and warmed the room upstairs. We were very excited to find we had a place to dress in upstairs that was warm.

Grandfather was quite noted for having the first thing of its kind in the community. He bought one of the first cookstoves, and grandmother said it was a real curiosity. There was a wonderful old fireplace in the kitchen, and grandmother told me it cost her a great many real efforts to get used to cooking on the new stove. For a long time, she would not allow the old fireplace to be dismantled, for she thought there could not be enough cooking done on a little cookstove for all our Thanksgiving company. By the time I came along, the fireplace was used for a storeroom, and its four doors, which folded upon themselves, were kept closed most of the time.

Grandmother also had the first sewing machine in York County. It was a Howe, and cost $150. It was the greatest of curiosities—people came for miles to see a "machine" sew.

In 1850, grandfather bought a melodeon for $200. It looked for all the world like a little kitchen table with drawers in it, but when the top was lifted, there was a keyboard. Mother has told me that little instrument was the most beloved thing in her life. It was just a shiny bit of furniture, but I remember how it was revered by all the family. Because we had music and because there were young people in our house, other young people came from miles around.

The house stood on the top of a short, rather steep, hill. At its foot was the run (creek). On its bank was the washhouse with all the then modern improvements. At one end was a big fireplace with a crane for three kettles, usually iron ones. At the other end was a built-in furnace with two fitted copper kettles, in which the cider and fruit butters were boiled. In this little house we did the washing, boiled the soap, butchered the hogs and beeves—events that to me were all full of interest. Close by the washhouse was a little brick building whose only openings were a door in one side and a hole in the roof—this was the smokehouse, where the meats were smoked and cured for the winter's use.

This hill and run bring to my mind many pleasant memories, especially of the winter, for there was not another site in all the country like it for coasting; after a snowfall, it was the scene of some wonderful times. The run was narrow, and the first freeze covered it with ice which would get thicker and harder with each cold spell; so when the snow came, it was all covered over and became a part of the meadow itself. We took our sleds to the top of the hill and there was nothing to interrupt us until we came to the fence a long way down.

Along the very crest of the hill were magnificent old walnut trees. When nutting time came, we always spoiled our clothing and stained our hands, preparing the nuts for winter. Standing under some of the trees was a bench with many holes in it, and there were wooden mallets to go with it. We filled our baskets with nuts and carried them to the bench, where we would lay them one by one over the holes, strike them with a mallet and break off the hull. This was thrown over the side of the bench, while the nut fell into a basket underneath. Nobody scolded us for getting dirty and I cannot remember that I ever worried lest my hands should never get white again, but I do remember exulting many times because my hands were the blackest or yellowest; that was proof I had hulled the most nuts and no achievement could exceed that.

On the opposite side of the house and on the level with it was the barn and what a big thing it was! It was a "bank barn" with three floors, granaries in the wings, with sheds beyond them and mows overhead. There were all kinds of stables and entries underneath the floors. It was a barn to play in, sure enough. Aside from the big barn, there was a special shed for the colts, a shed for the rockaway carriage, Uncle Rell's buggy and the sleighs; there was also an open wagon shed with corncribs on either side. There were a lot of pens for the hogs and pigs with a corn crib built in, and a chicken house and rabbit pen. Between the house and the barn were the pump and springhouse; they stood under half a dozen of the biggest honey locust trees I have ever seen. It was a veritable little village all by itself, and it was beautiful summer or winter.

The walks were all of flat stone, and over them everywhere were arbors, covered with grapevines from which we gathered many varieties of grapes. There was no wasted space. A group of sour cherry trees yielded bushels of fruit annually. The common black sweet cherry was plentiful, too, growing mostly along the public highways, but the oxheart was the choice among the cherries. It looked like the big fancy red cherry that comes into our markets now from California. We had three kinds of pears, a very early variety, then the commonest one and a late variety; the last sold for high prices on the market at Thanksgivingtime. We had apples all the year round. The cellar was filled with them in the fall, and many bushels were buried in the ground to be dug out fresh when the others were gone.

We had two big gardens. One was the vegetable garden, down by the run; it had an irrigation system that helped out a great many times in hot weather. Across the public highway from the front of the house was the berry garden, yielding currants both red and black; gooseberries, strawberries, red raspberries and tame blackberries. These latter were the show things of the place, very large, very sweet and quite uncommon. In the middle of this garden was a well, and over it a quince tree. Around the well for perhaps fifty feet or more, the ground was arranged into beds for flowers. These were edged with old boxwood, the prettiest green border there is, I think. In these beds were the peonies and these I loved better than anything else. We had a good many varieties and they were a joy to behold.

Yes, all this meant work and lots of it. It seems to me we did not have crop failures there as we do here, but I suppose we must have had. There always seemed to be plenty of everything and of course we were never allowed to let anything go to waste. Every member of the family learned to work to his utmost ability.

Mamma milked from ten to a dozen cows and made the butter and great quantities of cheese. I must tell you about the cheese. The kind most commonly known we called schmierkäse and we made this kind oftenest because it was the simplest to make and sold best. However, mother also made a cup cheese that sold, not so readily, but for much more money. She made it often in the winter, but never in the summer, because it had to be put to bed and kept warm. It was started just like schmierkäse; then the curds were put into tall, gallon crocks that were tied shut with paper and cloth. These crocks were put at the foot of the bed, between the feather beds, and we slept with them at night. After three or four days, the curds would be "rotted" and ready for the next steps—heating and seasoning. The cheese was then poured into cups to stiffen. A smooth, stiff substance emerged, pale and yellow, and really very palatable. We did not have much of it for our own use, but we had schmierkäse and apple butter to spread on our bread all the year round.

Mother or grandfather went to the Papertown and Harrisburg markets regularly—twice a week in summer, once a week in winter. It took a lot of things to make up a load for market as often as that, but we marketed every kind of thing and naturally learned to make use of all we had. We were obliged to be up early in the morning and we had no regular time for going to bed at night, for bedtime came when nothing was left uncared for that would go to waste. It meant work all the time, for that wagon had to be loaded and ready for its early morning trip. More than once I have picked forty quarts of berries in a day and gathered apples for cider until it seemed my back would never stop aching. Nobody meant to be unkind to us. In fact, our folks meant to do the very best that could be done for us, and I believe they did. We had delightful times together and much of everything that children like to have, and I know we had one of the most ideal homes that I have ever seen.

The old home held everything that was necessary but not many extras. We had rag carpet on all the floors but the kitchen, and sometimes in the winter there was one there, too. The carpet in the parlor differed from the others only in that it was all wool. The rag carpets were not hit-and-miss but were in stripes and blocks, and some of them were very pretty. They wore forever, too. There were no white curtains at the windows anywhere except in the parlor and spare bedroom. These were trimmed with homemade knitted lace and tied back with fancy tassels made of lamp wick, and I thought they were fine.

The parlor was furnished with the melodeon, a table filled with photographs, and six wooden chairs painted grass green and decorated with pink flowers. The body of the old carpet, which had already served for more than twenty years, was also green. There was nothing on the wall except one or two likenesses of dead babies; a few frames holding hair collected from all the relatives and fixed up with bits of flowers and ribbons; and a cornucopia. This latter was in the shape of a boot about two feet long; glued fast to it was everything one could think of on the earth or under it, and the whole thing was varnished. This hung on the wall as an ornament. The Lord's Prayer in a frame and a map of the United States were the only other decorations.

The walls were all white except for a border and some hand-painted flowers in the center of the ceiling and in the corners. These were added simply for the color, I suppose, for surely they did not look like anything in nature.

The chairs all over the house were of grandfather's own make, and some of them were very comfortable. In the sitting room we had a table, a bookcase and a corner cupboard, an old-fashioned grandfather's clock which showed the changes of the moon and the days of the month, the stove and the woodbox. The corner cupboard was built into the wall and was a wonderful place. It held everybody's work baskets, all the drygoods waiting to be made into clothes, etc., and the week's mending to be looked over and put back in the proper places.

There was one thing in that cupboard that I always wanted but never got, and I do not know what finally became of it. It was just a few yards of a bright-colored calico, in alternating stripes of red and brown, with a little vine running through the stripes. Grandmother never wrapped it up, so I was always seeing it and wishing for it. Her reason for not using it was this: she had bought it during the Civil War and paid seventy-five cents a yard for it; it was the one relic allowed on the place of those terrible days when things were very dear and money was scarce and people did not know what to do. I thought it would be great to have a dress made of it. The other girls would have been so envious, I knew. But grandmother said, in German, "This you cannot do. If you had it, you could not say it was worth seventy-five cents for it is only worth five cents a yard, and no more." This was the price of calico by the time I wanted it for a dress. I never could understand how *anything* could cost fifteen times as much as it was worth.

The woodbox was not taken away even when the new base-burner was put in to take the place of the old wood stove. It was a little higher than the chairs, and looked like a big box with a hinged lid.

It was almost as long as the side of the room between the door and the wall cupboard and was used as a lounge. I think I have rested as well on its hard top as I ever will on anything.

In the kitchen was the sink, painted yellow, the stove, two big cupboards—one to hold the milk in the cold weather—and the table. This table was a big thing and behind it was a long stationary bench, which seemed almost elastic; it accommodated any number of children.

The table was not set just as we set our table, but we always had all we could eat and the food was well cooked. Everything was put into big bowls and these were all set on the table at once; then they were passed around so that each person could help himself. If we did not get all we wanted, we had no one to blame but ourselves; then too we did not have to take anything that we did not want, and I like that idea. There was never an extra dish for anything; we put all the food on one plate. I shall never forget the first time I saw fruit put into a side dish and pie served on a plate by itself. I thought of how many dishes there would be to wash, and I am not sure but what this took away some of my appetite.

One thing we sometimes wanted and were denied was butter, because sometimes more was promised for the market than we could make; so when we ran short, we made it up by denying ourselves at home. I did not dislike the schmierkäse and apple butter, but I often wished there were not quite so many customers for our butter so we might have more of it at home.

We never had a tablecloth except on Sunday or when we had company. I never saw a napkin used until after I was grown, and it was a curious thing to me. I liked the idea very much and told mother about it and begged her to get some, but she said she could not enjoy her meals "with rags lying about" her plate. Some years afterward she bought some red napkins, and when I go home she tries to remember to put one at my place. Sometimes she forgets, and when she does she apologizes, but she has never cared to use them herself. So much for habit and one's early teaching.

My grandmother had a great big corner cupboard full of nice china, the real old-fashioned pinks and blues of more than a hundred years ago. They were in the room back of the kitchen, a room that was not used very much, and this china was brought out only on the big occasions when we needed a lot of dishes. I should like to have a few pieces of that china now.

The sleeping rooms, like the others, were supplied with just what they needed and nothing more. The spare room had a washbowl and pitcher, but nobody ever seemed to know it was meant for use. All the family washed and combed in the kitchen when it was cold, and when we could get outdoors we used a basin that stood on a bench near the cistern; it was kept there for just that purpose.

You will be interested in the beds we used to have.

We did not have mattresses, but used ticks such as my mother uses, out on the farm. She thinks, just as her mother did, that a bed would be neither clean nor comfortable if the straw was not changed every threshing time, and the tick given a good washing. That was what everybody thought in grandmother's old home in Pennsylvania. Once a year each tick was stuffed as tight as possible with new straw, and a big feather bed was placed on top of it. Such fun as we children had in those beds! And such trials with those feather beds when we were tired and out of sorts!

We climbed up on a chair and then into bed, always rolling and tumbling where we did not expect to go. The feather bed was used all summer, and the alternative, if it was too warm, was to take our pillows and stretch out on the floor. In the wintertime we slept with another feather bed on top of us. Grandmother took great pride in her "lovely live goose feathers," plucked by her own hand from the geese reared on the farm. To her, the use of chicken feathers suggested shiftlessness.

The spare room corresponded to what we know now as the guest room, but the only point of similarity was the bed. If you had looked into the spare room you would have seen that it was really a big storeroom, with all the contents in good order. Our bedrooms had no closets, so we hung our clothing on a row of hooks along one wall. The Sunday clothes for the whole family were in the spare room. A big chest in one corner held bags of dried fruit of every description. In another corner was a tall bureau, five feet high, something like a chiffonier, but wider and deeper. In these five or six drawers was the extra linen of all kinds, and the top was piled, tier on tier, with jelly glasses filled with goodies of every kind.

The bed was in another corner and at its foot was a washstand with the customary bowl and pitcher. The drawers were used to hold our collars and ribbons and such things, and the Sunday-go-to-meeting hats were piled one above the other in the cupboard part. The furniture was all mahogany. Two chairs and a rag carpet completed the room. There were dark shades at the windows which were always kept drawn to the bottom of the window unless there was company or it was cleaning day.

Years later mother went back to visit the old home. The same old things stood in their same old places. They lived just as they did years ago and years before that. How glad I am that we came away when we did! Mother was wiser than her fellows and she builded better than she knew. We children will bless her all our days. People fossilize in the same old place on the same old diet. I am glad I belong to the great "Wild West."

Chapter 5

THERE are many pleasant things to relate about our four years at grandfather's and perhaps it will make what I say more interesting if I begin with the members of the family.

Grandfather had always worked very hard and was fairly prosperous with enough for himself and his family and something to give to the needy. He had an inborn feeling, which he insisted on putting into practice, that all men are brothers, and it was his lifelong habit to help anyone he thought needed it if they asked him to do so.

I have heard grandmother say that she knew tramps were somehow aware of the fact that she would feed them, for they were always coming her way. There were a great many beggars in that country and they were never turned away from our house; if they asked for a night's lodging, they got that too. Grandfather said that we might be entertaining angels unawares, and I used to wonder what it meant and if any of the queer-looking people I saw would ever turn into angels. I do know that grandmother and mother used to grumble to each other about "Pap's crazy notions," but no matter how much they were inconvenienced, the beggars stayed overnight at least if grandfather was at home.

One night a good-looking fellow asked for his supper and lodging and spent the evening with the family. He entertained us very nicely and made an especially good impression on grandfather. His story was flavored with some pathos and he won such sympathy that he was put into the clean spare bed. Next morning after breakfast he went away. However, he left his card behind him. A few days later someone began to scratch and soon the whole family was scratching. It was wintertime and our family wore flannels—and they could not be boiled. What a siege of it mother had! It was not until spring that we succeeded in getting rid of the pests, which we called graybacks.

After that experience, mother persuaded grandfather that it was really unjust to the family for him to take people in so freely, and grandmother announced that if she had anything to say about what was to be done in that house, no more tramps would sleep there. So, after that, all those who came slept in the barn and were fed on the porch instead of at the table. Mamma used to say she knew the barn would be set on fire some night, but it never was.

Grandfather's education was limited, according to our present standards, but it was quite above the average for his day. He read well, wrote a good hand, and was considered a leading man in the community. He was a good thinker and planner and had ability to execute his plans. He invented a piece of machin-

ery which he called a clover huller. This, according
to all just rules, should have made him a rich man.
However, he was taken advantage of by men he
thought his truest friends, two or three of whom
grew rich from his invention. Grandfather not only
got nothing out of it but lost money besides. The
machine was a great success and for a number of
years the family was very annoyed because grandfather was so proud and happy about what he could
do with it that he insisted on traveling over the
country demonstrating its merits.

He was a good gardener and was known for miles
around as the best man to graft fruit trees. On his
farm he grew everything he could find room for, and
it was kept in model order. Everything had its place
and was kept there, and all work was performed at
its proper time.

Grandfather was never idle. The washhouse was
his workshop and there he kept his tools always
ready for use on any occasion. He had a shoemaker's
bench and mended all the shoes, but I do not think
that he ever made any. We all wore handmade shoes,
however, both for Sunday and weekdays, but these
were made by a professional cobbler.

When he was a boy, grandfather learned the
cooper's trade and made all the barrels he needed
for his own use. His "fill-in" work was making
baskets for all sorts of things. He brought white
oak wood from the mountains and did all this work
from start to finish by himself. A great many baskets
were used in his marketing, and if he made more

than he needed, there was no trouble in selling all
he could spare. The standard ones were bushel and
half-bushel sizes, but he made his own quart berry
baskets, too, and I think he had several hundred
of them. I still have one from the last lot he ever
made.

When we went to live with our grandparents,
all their children were married and gone except Uncle
Rell, who was next to the youngest. Aunt Kate,
the eldest, had four children and lived close by—in
fact, all the children lived within three miles of home.
Uncle Levi, a blacksmith and music teacher, had one
boy and an adopted daughter. Amos was a tanner,
with six children. Mother had her six, and next to
mother was Lavina, the pet of the family, with two
children. Uncle Albert, a carriage maker, was the
youngest; he lived in Petersburg and had two children. Later his wife died and he married a widow
with four children. I have never seen him nor any
of his family since.

I loved to go to see Aunt Lavina. She was very
small, in contrast to all the others, and she seemed
more like a chum to me than an aunt. I thought she
must have been more of a real girl than either mother
or Aunt Kate. She had prettier dresses and little
fancy things. I know now that it was only because
she was so much younger and that mother and Aunt
Kate had long since converted all their girlish vanity
into the practical common sense necessary to make
ends meet for their families. Aunt Lavina had a basket full of ribbons, just odds and ends. I do not sup-

pose there was any really worth-while thing in the
lot, but that basket was one of the envies of my life.
I have never, even to this day, seen anything that I
wanted so much to have for my own. It is a shame
that children's hearts go hungry for such little
things. How I wished and wished I could have ribbons like that and I longed for them and dreamed
about them! I thought when I grew to be a big girl
one of the things I would be sure to get for myself
was a basket of ribbons just like Aunt Lavina's. I
have never gotten them.

My grandmother's maiden name was Zinn. She
was the youngest of twelve children—six boys and
six girls—and on her fiftieth birthday, they were
all living. It is such a remarkable record that I like
to think of it.

Grandmother Heikes was just as good a manager as grandfather, and nothing ever suffered if it
was left for her to attend to. She seemed always to
be in perfect accord with grandfather's way of doing things and as far as I know, she may have been
the one who set the standard. I have learned by experience that the mother of the house has it in her
power to make her home as she wants it, even when
the father seems to be at the head.

Grandmother read her German Bible, but spent
no effort on any other reading matter. She could
not read or write a word in English. It was trying to
her always to have to make her mark when there
was a document to be signed. I could not see any ex-

cuse in the world for anyone being and *staying* so ignorant.

When we moved into grandmother's house, I was still proud of my experience in teaching Ellen Snyder to read, and I at once proposed to teach grandmother. She was past her sixtieth birthday, but she said we would take a little time each day for study. We did this, and in four years she learned to read her English Bible and was able to write her name. This was a great comfort to her through her last years.

She and I had some funny times getting our lessons, and sometimes we had hard ones, too. She was very anxious to learn and she did her best, but her English was very limited and I was only a child. She would spell a word with the English letters and understand what the word meant, but instead of the English pronunciation she would give it in German. "F-o-x" would be "fuchs"; "d-o-g," "hund"; "c-a-t," "katze." Sometimes I would just tell her about it and go right on, but there would come days when I would giggle and laugh until the dear old lady refused to read any more and sent me off ashamed of myself because I had hurt her feelings.

She was a dear, good grandmother and a kind friend but no one would have thought of calling her sweet, for she was very large—and weighed about two hundred pounds. Her voice was clear and authoritative, sometimes complaining and dissatisfied, though she never really meant to be. Her face was frank and beautiful; looking at her you could not doubt either her sincerity or her ability.

It was during our lessontimes that she gave me the most of herself in those four years. Sometimes we confined ourselves to the lessons, covering them as fast as we could. Other times we would have long talks together and I remember one that has helped me a great many times. I had a habit of talking too much. I said many things that I should not have said, and one day after one of my especially annoying spurts, she kept me with her after the lesson and urged me not to say such things. I argued that I might as well say them since I thought them, and that was just the same thing. She replied, "Oh, no, child, there is a lot of difference. You cannot help that the birds keep flying over your head, but you can keep them from building nests in your hair, and there is just *that* difference between the things that you think and the things that you say. Think about it for grandmother." I have thought about it many times and it has often helped a lot.

My grandmother, I think, fulfilled the most puritanical idea of a thrifty housewife. In her youth, everything was homemade and homespun, too. The flax was grown, and the linen was spun and woven; the sheep were raised and the wool made into cloth for clothing. I can remember piles of beautiful linen she still had on hand when we came away, and she told that she had ten chemises, ten pairs of drawers, ten nightgowns and ten white skirts when she was married, besides dozens of pillow slips and sheets and all her chaff ticks; and the interesting part of it was that she had woven, spun and made them all

herself. Her bed covers were all the homemade coverlets, so rare nowadays, and all her blankets were of
her own make.

These things were still in use when we were home,
and grandmother continued to spin her own thread
and make a few bolts of woolen cloth all her life.
"The stuff you buy isn't worth making up," she
said. Her spinning wheel had its season in the sitting
room every year. The whole household was fitted
out with stockings of her own knitting. In the winter, these were of wool and in the summer, of cotton.
Sometimes she knit them for us children with fancy
stitches.

When she was first married bread pans were not in
use. The bread was set to raise in tight round baskets
known as breadbaskets and, when ready to bake,
was thrown right into the oven on the ashes, after
the present fashion of baking the Vienna bread.
When pans came into use, grandmother adopted
those, so she had a lot of baskets on hand. I do not
think they could ever be worn out, they were so
sturdy.

These baskets found various uses; one of them
was for her sewing, another held her knitting. They
were kept on a certain shelf in the closet in the sitting
room. The moment she sat down, she began to knit
or to sew, and we were taught to do the same thing
—I always had to do my patch work. I would not
learn to knit, and I made so much fuss about it that
I was allowed to crochet instead, and during my life
I have done quantities of crocheting. I have since

learned to knit but have never made any stockings. I learned to sew, too, and after my fourteenth birthday made all the garments for mother, my sister Leah and myself. I always helped to make the pants for the boys but never did it quite alone. I am glad that I learned to do all these things when I was a child, for it has been of great benefit to me. I never learned to spin, but mother still has her wheel and keeps herself supplied with thread to mend with, or to sew anything when she "wants it to hold."

When I think of my childhood surroundings, it seems to me I would be a queer piece of humanity if I ever ceased to be wanting to do something. At our house the idea of "rest" meant to do the next thing that needed to be done.

Chapter 6

GRANDFATHER was a puritanical sort of Christian, and under no circumstances were his religious duties neglected. We never ate breakfast without first listening to a chapter of the Bible read by one of the older members of the family—usually grandfather himself. Mother kept up her family worship, too, but she was never so strict as her father was. Sometimes when she was very busy or too tired, she would just go to bed and say her prayers there. But not so my grandfather. After the reading he would start that dear old hymn—and I love it:

A charge to keep I have, a God to glorify,
A never-dying soul to save and fit it for the sky.

We would sing the four verses and then grandfather would pray, after which we would have our breakfast. My Uncle Rell used to get very much out of sorts sometimes and say that grandfather took pains to read the longest chapters and make the longest prayers on the mornings he had the most work to do. I am sure it must have been pretty hard for grandmother to have served a really palatable breakfast when it had to stand so long, but I do not remember that anyone ever complained about it. That was the way things had to be done.

Sunday was the hardest day in the week, for we went to church twice and to Sabbath school, too, and it was so easy to pick up someone to take home to spend the day and then take them back to church at night. I often heard my mother say she wished she could have just one Sunday alone, but I guess she seldom had it.

Before we could go to bed at night, Sunday or weekday, grandfather would get us all together in the sitting room and read a chapter from the Bible and comment on it. Then he would put aside his Book, wipe his glasses and strike up some familiar tune—some chorus with which we were familiar and to which he would fit innumerable verses. Sometimes it would not be a very long service, but at other times it seemed as if the mood would never end. The singing done, we kneeled at our chairs to pray. Grandfather would be the first to pray. Grandmother would follow, then mother, then the next oldest and so on, down to the smallest.

How sleepy we did get sometimes, and I have heard grandmother and mother say, "Pap, you make the children too tired," but evidently he thought it was the kind of discipline we needed and their admonitions never altered his way of doing. This case seems to prove the statement that early teachings are the ones that last, for every one of his seven children have followed most faithfully in his footsteps. My mother and my uncle have had many hard times here in the West, and often they have had to pull on alone, but they still believe their way of doing is the right way and the one which children should be taught. They are sure the children of the present day are being led very far from the paths of righteousness by the loose customs of the times (1899). Grandfather lived and practiced his faith most beautifully to the end of his life, and although he was unconscious for a week before he died, no one could have questioned that he was glad and ready for the final summons.

It was nearly three miles to the church we attended, and we went to prayer meeting each week all the year round. During the winter when a Protracted Meeting was in progress, all who could had to go every night. These were great occasions, and it was customary to go forward to the mourners' bench and "get religion." Some people used to go forward every year. Children went, too, lots of them, and I was talked to and had my sinful life set before me from all angles many times; but somehow, although I was often awed by the things that were said and done, I always had a feeling within me that something was wrong about it and I could not bring myself to go forward with the others. I had a feeling then, which has since become a conviction, that the sensational in our religious life is wrong—and having it in the church does not make it right.

The sect to which we belonged was the United Brethren. They were very much like the Methodists in their discipline and worship. I do not know in

what they differ except that the church of which I
am speaking kept the old custom of washing one
another's feet at the Communion Day services. This
I know the Methodist Church does not do. It was
always a funny affair to me, and it was particularly
amusing to us when we heard people remark that
somebody's feet smelled so bad they could hardly
stand to wash them. I was perfectly sure that I
would never join a church that kept up a custom
like that.

Communion was taken as the congregation knelt
about the altar rail in front of the pulpit, and there
were one, two or three tables or groups, according
to the number of people participating in the feast.

One of the truest signs that the Spirit was working among the good members was the series of shout-
ings they set up. Someone would "get filled with the
Spirit" and come away from the altar, perhaps
prancing up and down the aisles, and shout "Praise
the Lord!" or "Glory, Hallelujah!" or some other
such phrase. His eyes would be shut or turned to the
ceiling. Sometimes these inspired ones would trip
and fall over each other, or drop to their knees on
the floor, and oh, dear me!—such exciting times
as I have seen in those meetings. Whenever people
began to shout, I began to shrivel up inside. I felt
a strong desire to get up and hammer them. I
thought they needed just that.

Now and then, some member with more of the
Spirit than anyone else would "go into a trance"
and appear to be unconscious for hours or even a

day or two. This was a great state to attain, and the
person to whom it happened was paid much defer-
ence for a long time after. To go into a trance was
a sure sign that the person so privileged had attained
"sanctification" and would not sin any more, and it
was all very serious and done in great earnestness.
How could it be? I hated every bit of it and everything in me rebelled against it, but our folks thought
it was all right. And mother would weep even now
if I were to tell her how I abominated all that sort
of thing and thought it all a farce and that no good
could come to one out of it. It was grandfather's and
grandmother's religion, and they believed it and died
by it. Mother believes it, too, and sometime it will
take her to heaven just as it did her parents, but I
can never go that way. I hope to meet them all at
the end of the journey, but I cannot travel by the
same road.

Only once in all the years of attending protracted
meetings did my own family become the center of
excitement. Grandfather was always at the front
with his audible "Praise the Lord!" and "Glory,
Hallelujah!" but we knew just what to expect from
him. Grandmother never varied her ecstasies beyond
her repeated but quiet "Gott sei dank!" with perhaps an extra use of her handkerchief. As for mother,
she had a strong voice and was always a leader in
whatever music there was on any occasion. So it
came about that her part in the meetings was to select
the right thing to sing and to lead out for all the

congregation to follow. Her contribution was one of praise, and much of the success of the meetings depended on the spirit she put into the music.

However, one Sunday night we were in church in Buttstown, where the family attended regularly. Meetings had been in session for some two or three weeks. Things had been going fine; there were a dozen "seekers" at the mourners' bench. The minister gave a rousing talk on the sins that would take us to hell if we refused to repent and be saved. Grandfather was in his accustomed place, drumming up feeling with his stereotyped phrases. Mother was on the front seat of the amen corner with her singers. Everybody was singing and shouting, and mother repeated the choruses, standing up in order to get her people to follow her lead a little better.

I was halfway back in the little church and I soon realized there was unusual excitement but did not understand what it was about. However, I did notice that I had never seen mother act so in leading the singing. She fairly shouted the words and waved her hands to keep time. Then all at once something happened. Mother dropped her book to the floor and set her eyes on the ceiling and began to shout, "Glory, glory, glory, Hallelujah!" and clapped her hands. She repeated the performance over and over. She came around the altar in front of the mourners' bench and prayed for each one as she passed.

On across the front of the church she wandered until she came to the end of the altar on the opposite side from where she started. By this time, a half dozen people were shouting, and someone starting out from the other amen corner to which mother had wandered collided with her with such force that she was thrown to the floor. Some men tried to help her up and in the shuffle first one and then another was thrown on top of her. Frantic, I ran up to the front, thinking she would surely be killed and feeling that I must strike somebody for all this horrid nonsense.

Presently the pile unfolded, and mother came out serenely, thanking the Lord for all he had done for her. For many days afterward, reference was made to "the night that 'Manda got happy," but I always thought of the occasion as the most disgraceful thing I had ever seen, and I was ashamed that it had come to our family. In the community, mother was numbered among the notables. I was constantly afraid she would do it again and always thankful she never did.

The greatest event of all the year was the camp meeting. The church owned its own strip of woodland, and in August of each year we would gather together our camping outfit and spend from ten days to two weeks in the woods.

It was one of the keenest of delights to me to get ready for that annual occasion. I used to count the days! The directors would usually announce the date about six weeks before the opening, and it seemed to me these would never go by. No other time ever was so long, then or since, as were those

six weeks. Sometimes the individuals belonging to
our company numbered forty. The railroad was
about half a mile from the grounds, and excursions
from all points near and far brought large crowds
daily; the Sunday crowd often became a burden and
a nuisance. The same kind of meetings here in the
West would not be a success I suppose, but I do not
know. I would like to see it tried out.

The tents were placed in the form of a large circle.
They were of all sizes, according to the number of
persons who would occupy them. Our tent was
always a very large one because none of the relatives
took their own. They all expected to stop with the
grandparents when they came to camp. We had a
small tent back of the large one, for cooking purposes. There was a big boarding place—long tables
under a simple shed roof—where board could be had
most inexpensively and here the visitors used to get
their meals, so we did not often cook for outsiders.
We did little cooking on the grounds even for the
family, most of it being done at home and brought
to the camp.

Inside this tent circle was an improvised pulpit
and a number of seats, and there the services were
held. There were meetings of all kinds at nearly all
hours of the day. The truly devout attended them
all, but some did not want to, and the children were
not expected to go to any of them regularly except
the one arranged for them, which was called the
Children's Hour.

You never could guess the good times we had—

not at the meetings, but all over the grounds and everywhere. Sometimes a bunch of us would gather behind one of the tents and tell stories, and now and then make so much noise that someone would come and scold us or perhaps scatter us to the winds. But we never despaired. We did the same thing back of some other tent in a little while. The woods were full of swings, and the entire place was kept just like a big park, so that it really was a great outing, and I feel now that I had a genuine vacation every year.

We gave credits for the best story each day; and the narrator of the best one could tell another story on the next day. One day I told this story:

"When my grandmother was a little girl, she lived in the country, way off from the road, and you had to go down a long lane to get to the road. On each side were big trees close together and the tops reached together overhead, and under all the pretty trees there were seats, all kinds of seats. When it was daytime, it was *beautiful,* and when the moon shone bright it was nice, too; but when it was pitch-black dark it was *awful*. But it was the only way to get to grandma's house and everybody had to go that way. Grandfather was a young man and he was going over to grandmother's house to see her quite often, and sometimes when grandmother had her work all finished up and was dressed in a fresh gingham or calico dress, she would walk down the lane to meet grandpa and then sometimes they would sit under the trees and talk all evening and have such

a good time. One very dark night she started and
went only a little way when she saw a woman all
dressed in white. Grandma ran back home in a hurry.
Pretty soon grandpa came and she wanted to tell
him about it because she thought of course he must
have come right by the woman, but she did not say
a word. The next night she went to meet him again
and there was that woman all in white walking toward her. Grandmother ran home and this night she
told grandfather and they walked up to the end of
the lane but saw nothing. On the next night she
went to meet grandfather and there was the woman
again, dressed in white. She was moving her arms.
Grandmother was so dreadfully frightened that she
told her mother about it, and her mother went with
her and, sure enough, they both saw the woman
waving her arms. Grandmother's mother said, 'It's
a spirit and someone is surely going to die in this
family inside the next six months.' And do you
know, in about two months one of grandmother's
cousins died!"

This is a true story and was told to me by a maid
who lived with my grandmother for seventeen years
and knew lots of wonderful stories. But it wasn't a
ghost after all, only a big scarecrow that one of
grandmother's brothers had dressed up in some old
wheat sacks and put near some of the cherry trees to
keep the birds away. The day before the last night,
one of the girls who had been picking cherries tore
her big apron so badly that, just for fun, she put it

on the scarecrow, putting sticks in the sleeves to make them stand straight out. When the wind blew the apron, grandmother and her mother both thought the figure was moving, but it wasn't at all —and there wasn't any ghost. But *anyway*, grandmother's cousin died, and I believe the Passover Angel just hid behind the scarecrow and told them she was going to. The children all liked that story and I would tell it over and over.

Another favorite was:

"One night when my mother had come home from going over the mountains to Papertown to market, she was awfully tired and hungry. I should have done the milking and hunted the eggs, but I had not done it. Mother said I should go to the barn and hunt a few eggs so that she could make a little supper before she milked and fed the pigs. I ran out to the barn and was going into the stable, where I was sure I would find some eggs, but when I opened the door I saw something all white with two big, burning eyes looking at me, and I ran back to the house and told mother. She said Howard was to go with me and she knew there was nothing to be afraid of, but when we got to the door the thing came moving toward us and we turned and ran to the house faster than we ever had before, and told mother we had seen something terrible and it was coming after us. She said she had half a mind to make us go back alone again, but we were badly scared, and she knew we were. So she went with us

and when we all looked into the dark stable together, we saw the white apparition with the shining
eyes. It would move toward us a little way and then
back from us and then toward us. Mother said,
"That's funny," and walked inside the door. Out
came the bright eyes right at us, and it was our big,
old tomcat. Another step brought out our pet billygoat, that had been lying in the back of the stable,
and the "white thing" continued to move rapidly
to and fro. With a few steps more, mother put her
hand on the swaying thing, and touched the pillow
and the white sheet that we had taken to the barn
to lay the baby on while we played on the barn
floor that afternoon. We had had the idea of making
a swing and then we piled the things into the swing
and forgot all about them. Tom had gone to sleep
on the pillow, and when we had opened the door
the first time, Billy had gone in, touched the swing
in passing and had lain down on the straw to go to
sleep. And we had come out in time to find the
swing still moving. So there you have a really truly
ghost story."

Chapter 7

IT does seem strange that more attention was not paid to education in our section of the country. All the people in the community seemed to be in comfortable circumstances with nice homes, although there was no particular elegance anywhere. But no importance was placed on schooling.

When mother was a little girl, there were not more than three or four months of school a year, and the pupils were taught by someone in the neighborhood—usually the one bidding the lowest fee. As a result of that system, not one of my aunts or uncles had an education. Uncle Rell did take a short course at some normal school, but I think it was hardly equal to the eighth grade. They got the best education they could, or so they believed, and grandfather had the largest library in all that country, though it would not seem like a library to us today. In the sitting room was a bookcase with three shelves containing about forty or fifty volumes. They were all "subscription books," and that meant that they dealt either with religion or agriculture. I read all of them that I could and more, too. When I think of all the work that had to be done all through the week, and the limited education of every

member of the family, it seems surprising that there
were books of any kind.

The folks were very proud of my ability to read,
and we spent many an evening around the table—
grandfather weaving baskets, grandmother knitting,
mamma sewing—while I read Bible stories or criti-
cisms, or perhaps something from the weekly paper.
When we came away, grandfather made a great
sacrifice, giving me his favorite storybook to bring
along to Kansas, with the injunction that I should
never cease to read it. It's title is *Young People's
Bible Stories*. Up to now—1899—I have not failed
to follow his advice, for in truth I find it explains
the things it touches better than any other book I
have found since.

The schoolhouse in our district was known as
Rocky Ridge. It was a small brick building, with
three windows on either side and a lean-to coal shed
that shut out the light from one of them. A big
stove stood in the center of the room and a row of
seats on either side. The teacher had a little platform on which was a hollow-backed desk, where he
sometimes put bad boys for punishment. The building was quite an old one and stood in the heart of a
woodland. There were many rocks about the
grounds and a running stream with logs and moss
and vines and trees of all kinds. It was a beautiful
place for a country schoolhouse.

We had five months of school and nobody wanted
to miss a day—I never did. We walked about a mile
to school, and followed a path through the fields.

When it was wet or rained, we were taken in the buggy. We had a great deal of snow in the winter-time, and sometimes our feet and hands got pretty cold. As long as the snow was not too deep, Howard would lead the way and make a path because he wore boots. The rest of us put old stocking legs over our shoes and when we got to the schoolhouse we were not wet at all. Sometimes, on very cold days, grandmother would make a big thick pancake, wrap it in paper and then wrap it about our hands with a piece of cloth. We called it our "pancake muff" and were always delighted to have it.

There were days when the snow was too deep for us to walk, and then Uncle Rell would hitch the horse to the bobsled, put on the sleigh bells and take us to school. That was the most fun of all, especially going home. We would start from the schoolhouse with all the children who could pile on, and everyone going our way managed to find a place somehow. If the day was very cold he took us straight home and no fooling, but if the day was nice and he could spare the time, he would drive a little way in good order, then all at once the horse would shy to the side and over would go the sleigh. Such yelling and squabbling as there would be, get-ting loaded onto the sleigh again. Then a little ride farther and perhaps we all went over again. I have known him to dump us into the snow half a dozen times in one evening, and we loved it. We had so much fun, we were always sorry when he did not take the time to have a snow romp with us.

I loved my school and my teachers, but now and then I was greatly tried. I think it is most unfortunate to have a precocious child brought constantly before the public. I was a very little girl compared with the others in the class, and as I think of it now, it seems every teacher liked to show me off; at any rate I was constantly being asked to read or spell or analyze a problem or put work on the board. If any of my children show signs of forging ahead of the other pupils, I know one thing—I shall be after the teacher who urges them on.

Our folks at home did not understand, and every night I had to bring home my books and study. It was no task for me, for I loved it, but everybody helped me keep right at it. Night after night I recited my lessons, and often no one understood anything about the matter in hand, but I went through with it. I spelled through every book that Uncle Rell could find words in to spell, and then he bought a Webster's *Academic Dictionary* and we spelled all the words in that. But perhaps it was for the best, after all, for if I had not gotten a little education while I was young, I would not have had any at all. And I took great pride in pleasing my teachers and my people.

There were five schools in our district, and on the first Friday of each school month there was an "institute" at one of the schoolhouses. Every teacher and pupil of the other four schools had to attend. The school visited gave its regular program, and the visiting teachers heard recitations all the forenoon, while the visiting pupils were supposed to benefit by what they heard. If a teacher was absent, he lost his pay for that day. In the afternoon the program varied, usually consisting of recitations from the best pupils and talks by the teachers or members of the school board.

After recess in the afternoon, there was always a spelling match, to see which school could spell down all the rest. The last two years our school won all the institute tests, for during that time I was never spelled down. There were also night spelling matches all over the country to which I was invited, and though the weather was often bad, it was never too bad for Uncle Rell to take me. The last winter I went a great deal and won the distinction of being the best speller in the county for I never missed a word. I was only fourteen and I think now, considering my indulgence by teachers and home folks and my hard-earned success, that my pride was perhaps pardonable. Constant practice makes a success of almost anything, and I certainly was kept at it.

On one of these institute occasions, early in our last winter in Pennsylvania, I wanted to wear my Sunday dress and shoes. I had taken a fancy to a certain big boy, and I thought he rather liked me. I wanted to look my very best; so I begged to be allowed to fix up, but grandmother would not permit it. I had to go in my usual garb. I went away from home crying about it and cried more or less all day. I made mistakes in all my recitations except spelling, and it is a wonder I did not miss there, too.

When I got up to read, the tears overwhelmed me, and I was sent to my seat in disgrace. I could not read aloud again that winter. When I tried, my heart would begin to jump and tears were sure to follow. How I dreaded the reading lesson no one can know. It came first in the morning after opening exercises, and one morning I played about until after class and told the teacher I had to go to the shoemaker's. He was a very good teacher and he guessed that I was telling him an untruth. He kept at me until I told him all about my dread, and he believed me and excused me from reading until I felt that I wanted to try it again. It took me a long time, and it was a hard struggle for me to get back to where I could read in public again.

We carried our dinners to school and had fine times playing together through the noon hour. We played the same old games, many of them, that the boys and girls play now: Tig-ring, Baking Bread, Town Ball, Jenny Jones, Bingo, Button, Old Policeman, Drunken Sailor, Prisoner's Base, Andy-over, London Bridge, What O'Clock and others. Nothing was more generally enjoyed than snowballing and washing each other's faces.

Two things stand out in my memory in connection with my school days at Rocky Ridge. The first had to do with some flying squirrels that made their home in the loft. They got in through a broken window that was never fixed from year to year, and the place was filled with them. They annoyed us in school hours and now and then some of the braver boys were allowed to climb through the opening in the ceiling and drive out some of the pests. One noon, when the teacher had gone away, some boys went up into the loft and caught half a dozen of the squirrels and brought them down into the school-room. For a little while, they entertained everybody who was there; then some one suggested playing a trick on the teacher. We put them under the water bucket on the teacher's desk, and everybody kept mum when he came into the room.

The trick worked fine. He came in a little late, hurried and perhaps worried, too, for someone in his family was ill and that was the reason for his absence. He walked to his desk, saying, "John, put this bucket where it belongs," at the same time putting out his hand and picking up the bucket to give to John. The fun that followed cannot be expressed. Those six frightened flying squirrels, in a room with a dozen nervous girls and as many teasing boys, produced the biggest kind of a circus, and half the afternoon was played away trying to get them outside of the building.

Another vivid memory has to do with the way in which we sang and chanted our Geography. I learned the capital cities of every state and country by singing or chanting them, and for years afterward I wanted to sing when I tried to think of the capital of any place. An illustration follows for the New England states:

Maine, Augusta, is on the Kennebec river,
New Hampshire, Concord, is on the Merrimac river,
Vermont, Montpelier, is on the Onion river.
Massachusetts, Boston, is on the Boston harbor,
Connecticut, Hartford, is on the Connecticut river;
Rhode Island has two capitals—Providence and Newport.

We repeated each line twice before going on to the next. Imagine how funny it sounded. We covered the United States, South America, Europe, Asia and Africa in just the same way. Some of the tunes changed a little but never the plan.

My best chum in those days was my second cousin, Lillian Heikes. She was a very pretty girl and fond of the boys. Her chief delight was in having a beau, and she had them. One Saturday evening not long before we went away from grandfather's, she asked me to come and spend the night with her. Her folks were away and she asked two boys to spend the evening with us. If my mother had known of the plan I could not have been there, but she didn't. We had a good time, of course. Will Weaver, the boy who had come to be with me, asked if he might walk home from church with me on Sunday evening. I knew I would have to ask my mother about it before giving an answer.

Up to this time I had not learned to comb my hair. When I very bashfully asked my mother if the young man might come home with me, she said, "The very idea of a girl wanting to have beaux when she can not comb her own hair!" Then she said she would think about it. After awhile she said,

"If you do not ask me to comb your hair any more, you may come home with Will." I never worked harder at anything in my life than I did at trying to put up my hair through the following week. It was quite long and very heavy, but I never asked mother to comb it again.

We all attended Sunday school every Sabbath afternoon in a church near home. The service was held expressly for all the children of the country around. Preaching services were held in various denominational churches throughout the district. Until this time I was very happy with my brothers and quite willing to assume the care of them anywhere, but somehow this winter I hated to "sit all in a row" with them. There were too many of us. I wanted to sit with the big girls instead, and do the things that they did. One of the features of Sunday school in those days was the committing to memory of questions and answers on the Bible and learning Bible verses. I did a lot of it every year and always won whatever prize was offered. This last winter I objected and did not want to do it, I wanted to teach instead, but was not allowed the privilege. My last Sunday school work as a pupil was committing the Psalms. I learned a great many verses and whole chapters, but I cannot repeat many of them today.

At Christmastime the Sunday school gave an entertainment and mother had the leading part in the anthem that was sung for the occasion. It was the Twenty-fourth Psalm. I do not imagine that it was the rendition that impressed me, because music seldom has since, but somehow the phrases, "Lift up your heads, O ye gates; and be ye lifted up ye everlasting doors; and the King of Glory shall come in"; and then, "Who is this King of Glory?" have never ceased to speak to me. I can see that chorus now and hear my mother's voice above all the rest as it sounded that night. She seemed a real herald of the words she sang. I have told her since that I learned the meaning of an anthem that night, that it was a piece of music with only a few words that you sang over and over again and could never forget, and she said, "I guess that is what an anthem *ought* to be, but I think it very seldom is." I am sure now that she was right. How little we know the things we do or say that become mileposts in the lives of those about us.

During the last two years at grandfather's I attended what we called a summer school, that is, a spring term of two months, in a school about two miles from home. The teacher was a Miss Mattie Adams, and she was a great figure in my life. I thought she was beautiful. She did take a great deal of interest in her pupils and thought of many things to do that pleased us.

The schoolhouse was just across the road from the graveyard where my father was buried, and somehow his memory spurred me on to do my best. I would often look out of the window at his tombstone and wonder if he knew how hard his little girl was trying to study, partly to please him, so she might teach school some day as he had done.

On the first day of May each year, Mattie took us to the woods for a May Day party. We had a May Queen adorned with the flowers we gathered, and we ate our dinner under the trees. I have often had picnics in the woods since then, but through my whole life those two May Day parties have never been surpassed for gaiety.

Mattie wrote me the first letter I ever received with my own name written on the envelope, and for many years it was one of my treasures. The advantage and influence of first things is great. I shall never forget the conversations and recitations we had together. I do not agree with her teaching principles, for she encouraged me to commit Barnes's *History of the United States* to memory—a thing that I would now most seriously condemn. But she was a very true woman, and that means more than anything else. I think she is still unmarried and taking care of someone more lonely and helpless than herself.

A great amusement for the young people was what we called "flittings." It was a moving from one home into another, always in the springtime. The family that was going to change residence made great preparations for the occasion and invited their friends to be present, just as we invite our friends to come to a party. When the day came the host and hostess hired wagons enough to haul everybody who came. We gathered at the place which was about to be vacated and saw the goods loaded into the big wagons. Then the guests would hurry away to the new place and begin preparations for the dinner. The invited guests were supposed to assist the hostess in all she had to do, so the new home would be livable before they departed. I suppose that most of the time there were enough good, staid folks to do it, but the younger people never failed to have a good time. It was customary to go home after nightfall, and that was the signal for singing all the songs that anybody in the crowd knew; we would sing and yell until we were hoarse, just as boys and girls do nowadays at a football game.

In the same way, public sales were made real social events. All the boys and girls in the neighborhood and nearby country would be on hand for the occasion, not because they expected to buy anything more than perhaps candy and oranges—but because they wanted to see each other, have a good time and enjoy the "eats."

When anyone in the country built a new house or a new barn, a day was set for what was called the "raising." The whole neighborhood was invited to come and help, and just as with the "flittings," the work was done by a few while much the larger part of the crowd enjoyed the social and the refreshments. Corn huskings, which were always held on moonlight nights, were also wonderful parties, but I was not old enough to participate in them before we left the old home. Two by two the shocks of corn were to be husked, and then all would go to the house for apples, cider, pie, or cake and lots and lots of fun. Sometimes the girls could throw out more corn than the boys, and how they would gloat over the victory! Girls can do most things that boys can, and many of them can do things better and quicker. I am sure of this, but just the same I was often sorry that I was not born a boy.

Chapter 8

THERE were so many happy seasons. Perhaps whortleberry or huckleberry time was the best. These berries grew only on the mountains. It was over three miles from home to where we had to go to gather them. The way was uphill, among large and small stones, with here and there a clear running spring, lots of low brush and clinging vines. It seems to me the way was most romantic and it must have been very beautiful. I did not think of it then, for I was only concerned in getting to the place where the most berries grew. We usually gathered a good, big party and started very early in the morning. We would drive as far as we could, then leave the horse with the wagon and the lunch and climb up the hill—and it was always *up a hill*. Sometimes we would be very successful and come back loaded with the mountain fruit, but at other times we did not do so well. Now and then we would lose some member of the party and have quite a time calling and hunting for him. The berries grew on small, as well as on tall, bushes and there were both blue and black ones. The finest patches were in the clearings where the trees had been cut away. I always loved this outing. We seldom went back up the hill after eating our lunch by a nice cold mountain spring, but we went berrying a number of times in one season.

The foothills were full of wild blackberries, and we made many trips for these in a good year. A little later these hills were full of hazel nuts, and chinquapins, and we hunted for these, too. On the mountains in some localities there were a great many chestnut trees, and at least once every year and sometimes oftener, after a good heavy frost, we would get on our oldest rigs, and with an ax and bags would set out with Uncle Rell for the mountain. He would cut some good clubs, then climb the tree and pound on the limb as hard as he could. Down would come the chestnuts for us to pick up. Sometimes when a tree was full, he cut it down. This was always fine sport, and the one who did not cry when the falling burrs stuck him was very brave; and he who went home in the evening without "sticking all over," for the same reason, was quite in luck.

Nobody ever needed to sigh for a place to walk or something to do there. The mountains were whole storehouses in themselves, and supplied us with all kinds of pines, with cones in endless variety, as well as herbs and leaves. But the mountains did not provide quite so much pleasure, really, as the little woodlands that were so plentiful everywhere. They afforded amusement almost the year around. Early in the spring we began to rummage through them for flowers and mushrooms; a little later, the real mountain teawintergreen, with its beautiful red berries—greeted us. There were always birch and slippery elm trees. Flowers never failed, and the quantities of different plants, the various shapes and sizes of the leaves and all the other interesting things too numerous to be recorded, even if I remembered. Perhaps the laurels were the most beautiful of all the bushes, with their gorgeous flowers, something like the oleander. Everybody loved the laurels.

The wild strawberries were also a joy to us. We insisted they were sweeter than the tame ones and easier to pick (we were *obliged* to gather the tame ones), because it was so much fun to *hunt* for them. The haws and the May apples were two more things we liked to gather. We often tore our clothing in a mad race to get them, for they were always among the bushes. Mulberry trees grew near the woods too, and as the berries had no market value, these trees were exclusively our possession.

Some of the farm activities were interesting, too. As soon as the apples began to fall, they had to be gathered. The first ones were fed to the hogs. Later, when they began to ripen, they were picked over and the good ones made into cider for the market. Then whole trees were shaken, and a wagon was driven into the orchard, filled, and then driven to the cider press from which barrels of cider returned. Some of this was sold at once and some of it set for vinegar. Two or three times each season we made apple butter, barrels at a time. On the day the men made the cider, the women would *snitz* apples—that meant peeling, quartering and coring them. Sometimes friends would be invited for an evening to help at this, for there had to be from six to ten bushels of apple *snitz* ready for the boiling on the morrow.

On boiling day, the women were up at two or three o'clock to build the fire in the furnace in the wash house and get the cider on to boil. They boiled down the cider first—how long that took I do not know—and after awhile the apples went in as fast as they would boil down. There were two enormous kettles, and as soon as the apples were put in, the stirring began. The stirrers were made of boards about four inches wide, with many holes bored into them. To them were attached long handles so the person stirring could stand as far from the heat as possible. Once the stirring began it could not be interrupted for butter must be kept boiling all the time, and as it boils it thickens and sticks to the kettle. Somebody was always cross if the butter stuck. When we finished by midnight, we thought we were doing pretty well; it often took longer. One boiling made from thirty to forty gallons of light brown butter, which was carried to the garret for winter use. Peach and pear butter were made in the same way, but never in such quantities. The selling price in the markets was from eighty cents to one dollar a gallon.

Butchering day was another time when all the house was in a turmoil. One man, known as the butcher, did the killing for everyone in the surrounding country, and the dates had to be set far ahead. The butchering was usually done at our house before Thanksgiving, so that all other fall work could be completed by that time. There were from ten to twelve hogs, a beef and sometimes two, and now and then a lamb. On this morning, the folks were up early enough to have all the work done, breakfast over, and barrels filled with boiling water, ready to begin work at the first streak of dawn. Outside of the shop a large hogshead was fixed in a framework and connected to a platform, where the hogs were first scalded and then scraped. (They were killed at the barn and wheeled to the wash house.)

After the scraping, they were hung on gamut sticks in a place specially prepared, until all were worked over to the same point. Then everybody began to work. The butcher cut up the hogs, trimmed the hams and shoulders and put all the different pieces in the proper place. The women cleaned skins for the sausages. By ten o'clock the kettles were full of boiling meat; the chopper was cutting sausage meat; everybody was busy, and this kept up way into the night.

It usually took a week to get all the work finished. The lard and tallow had to be rendered next, and then it took a long time to pickle and smoke such pieces as required it. But it never grew uninteresting to me. This work provided meat for the year: Forty or fifty hams and shoulders; bushels of sausages, bolognas and chipped beef; gallons of crepples and headcheese; tripe and "little pigs," several hundred pounds of lard, and tallow enough for candles until the next butchering time. Now and then some of the hams and lard could be spared for market, but as a rule all this was "for our own use."

Another busy time came when grandfather "robbed the bees," rigged up in a very queer outfit. He put a big, round screen over his hat and tied a frill at the bottom of it, tightly around his neck. His gloves and coat sleeves were tied down together, also his pants and shoes. Then he took hive after hive, and as fast as he took out the honey, he brought it to the porch and brushed off the bees. Some of the women would take the honey into the house where the bees could not find it. Sometimes we had a hundred pounds to take care of at once.

It was fun for the children to have the bees swarm, but I know now what a lot of anxiety it must have given my mother and my grandmother. They were always on watch to see that they would not go away and be lost. Sometimes the bees came out nicely, and when they did we ran for tin pans kept for the purpose and made all the noise we could with them. If they settled on a limb low enough for mother to reach, she would saw off the limb and hive them herself. At other times they would seem to be out of humor and come out determined to go away, and then grandmother would ring the old dinner bell and bring the men to the scene of action. Sometimes they caught the bees and sometimes they did not; and sometimes even after they were in the hive, they would come out and fly away to the mountains, where people would rob them of the wild honey.

Howard, Dave and I were quite fond of robbing bumblebees and we did it lots of time. Of course we got stung, but we did it anyway. We liked to catch the "whiteheads" and tie strings to them and let them fly to see how high they would go. It was such fun to pull them in again.

One of our experiences with the bees occurred one day when I was left to care for Noble, who was just beginning to walk. I took him out behind the wood-shed, not very far from the bee stand, and amused myself by building a playhouse with sticks of fire-wood. Noble was being a good baby and playing around me, but I got too interested in building my house and forgot to watch him; suddenly I heard him cry. The sound came from the bee house. Sure enough, he had wandered to the front of the stand and evidently put his little fingers into some of the openings. The bees were very angry and although I took him away just as fast as I could, he had been stung in several places. There was no older person about the place and I did not know what to do.

How that baby did scream and pitch himself about! It was almost impossible for me to hold him. I tried soda and salt and soap to soothe the stings, but nothing helped. When I noticed his face puffing up like bread dough, I was terribly frightened. I dragged him back and forth from the house to the porch and cried with him, until finally mother came. There was great distress about Noble, and I was roundly scolded and sent upstairs to stay alone awhile as punishment for my negligence. His eyes were swollen entirely shut and his lips were so big he could not eat; his entire face was unrecognizable. Every little finger stood out stiff and straight as a stick, and he was a sick baby for awhile.

When mother called me later and said I could come downstairs if I would stop crying I said I could not see to come, for I was crying because I hurt all over. No one had paid any attention to me in the fright over Noble, but I had been stung, too. I never played near the home of the bees again. Some lessons cost a good deal, but they usually make a correspondingly lasting impression.

Howard was never afraid of anything for one minute, and to me he seemed a real hero. One day when we were playing in the run he caught a tiny water snake and ran after me with it. I set up a great shout and ran for the house. Mamma made him kill it, but he crept up beside me and said, "You were mean to tell, and I'll catch worse things than that and put them on you. See if I don't." But I liked to be with him anyway and he liked to have me unless he wanted to do something he did not want me to know about.

A few times during the summer, Uncle Rell and grandfather would make long pine fagots and, on a favorable evening follow along the run with their gigs—sharp forks with long handles—fishing for eels. They also carried a seine, which they used in certain holes to catch the fish. We always went along, and I wonder today if the excursions were not made largely for our pleasure. Sometimes they would have good luck and bring in a big catch that would perhaps take half the next day to clean. That part of the sport belonged to the women and children, and I think none of us enjoyed it as much as we did the fishing, but grandfather said the two went together and the work had to be divided. We ate all we could and the rest of the fish would be salted away in crocks for other meals.

Grandfather's farm was divided up into a number of small fields. I do not remember how many there were. They were separated from each other by two kinds of fence—worm (or rail) and post. Post fences were superior but also more expensive, so naturally the former predominated throughout the country. Our farm had the distinction of having almost all post fences. These wood fences had to be taken care of, and there was always some fence that needed fixing.

Crops were rotated, that is, something different would be grown in each field every year, in order that the soil might be made as productive as possible, and all the manure that could possibly be accumulated through the winter was hauled into the fields in the spring. During the winters one or more of the fields was always covered with lime which was brought from a limekiln several miles distant.

Often the plowing could not be done until the stones were removed, so there would be days and days of stone picking. It always seemed to me that the stones grew, for we would go over and over a field, putting as many stones as we could find in little

piles. When the field was covered with these piles—
they were put as far apart as possible so that the
team wouldn't have to stop too often—the stones
were gathered into a wagon and dumped into some
hollow place that needed to be filled. I realize now
how much more work had to be done on those fields
than is necessary in Kansas.

In grandfather's home there had been four sons
and three daughters—one boy and one girl were
older than mother, It was easier for grandmother
to get on with one girl to help in the house than for
grandfather to farm with one boy, so mother was
delegated to help her father do the farming. So it
came about that she had lived outdoors, doing everything the men did. In her day there was no reaper to
cut the wheat. It was done by men using cradles—
long knives with a framework attached—that threw
the grain into long rows. Other men followed the
cradle, gathered up a bundle of the grain and, with
a band made from some of the straw, tied it together.

Mother used to follow the cradle along with the
men and grandfather said she could make a better
stack of hay or grain than any man in the country.
I know that in most cases it is not right for a woman
to work so hard, but mother said she always preferred the out-of-door work to a day of hard housework. She never felt it was too much for her because
she loved to do it. It was this strenuous use of her
muscles in her early life that made it possible for
her to carry on the great task of her life in the West.

We children were all too small to help with the

farming, except to help pick stones, and we played too much to do even that well. We did our share toward all of it, however, in carrying out the lunches and water to the men who were at work. Twice a day, in the middle of the forenoon and again in the afternoon, we carried out a basket of good things to eat and jugs of water. When we arrived on the scene with our refreshments, everybody stopped work for a little rest, and we always had our "piece" with the workmen. We liked that.

Another hard task for the women was soap boiling. We always had a grease pot in which we saved everything that had a bit of grease on it, and down at the shop was a big tub known as the lye tub. When it was time to make the annual supply of soap, this was filled with wood ashes and straw. Water was poured on top of it and drained through very slowly into a tub; this was called lye.

When enough lye had been collected, the boiling began, and we made hard soap and soft soap and soap that was of neither kind. Sometimes it would not "turn to soap," and this was very annoying. Work went on until all the fat was consumed, and then there were great piles of soap to store in the old garret. Until I grew up I never knew what toilet soap was for I never had had any but homemade. I often hated the odor of it, but it didn't occur to me to protest about this.

Dyeing time was full of hard work and anxiety, too. Grandmother could not quite bring herself to use ready-dyed yarns. Factories did not make the kind of blue she wanted, so to the end of her days she kept her dye kettle and colored her own stocking yarns.

We had some of the nicest pets that any children could have, and, in each case, came to have them under most peculiar circumstances. Uncle Rell had a spirited young horse named Lady that he kept for his own driving purposes. He was very proud of Lady and thought no one else could drive her; we were warned to keep away from her heels and her head, for he said she would kick and bite. Children do not always mind, however, and one day when Lady was hitched to the buggy and tied to the post in front of the gate, something happened.

Uncle Rell heard her pawing the ground and hurried out to see what was the matter, but he did not find out until he was outside the gate. There was Elmer with both arms around her front leg, "loving her," he said, just as hard as he could. The horse could not put her head down on account of the checkrein, but she made no objection whatever save to paw the ground with her other front foot. Not many days after this, Lady was turned out of the stable, and finding the barnyard door open, she took a canter down the road. We children were playing under some willow trees by the creek and ran for the fence, but Lady stopped running and walked up to us as much as to say, "I love you and want to play with you." All four of us caught the mood at once and had not a bit of fear. That horse rubbed her nose all over us and we patted her neck and stroked her mane until Uncle Rell found us. After that we were allowed to drive her in the buggy and hitch her to our sleds and none of us was ever hurt.

Then we had a big, long-haired white dog named Joe. Uncle Rell had raised him and said he was the best watchdog in the country. He was about six years old when we went to live with grandfather, and for awhile the folks were afraid he would hurt some of us for he had never had children about him. At first he growled a little but later followed us everywhere. When we were left alone, Joe was given orders to stay with the children and take care of them, and I am sure he did it most ably more than once.

He lived to be fifteen years old, but grandmother said he grew lazy after we came West and stayed in the house most of the time. Uncle Rell wrote about him in his letters saying, "Joe wants Fatty and Pink (Noble and Leah) to come and pull his tail," or "Joe says he wants Davy to go for the cows and take him along," or "Joe would like to go with Flolly to see Lizzie (a neighbor girl)." We always liked that part of the letter best.

Not long after going to grandfather's we wanted some rabbits and were allowed to get a pair. One was gray, wooly as could be, and we named him Wooly. The other was a pretty smooth-haired, white and black one and we named her Grace. The experiences that we had with those rabbits would fill a book, and it is true that eighty rabbits altogether came from that one pair of rabbits. They

ate a load of stuff, and it was no small task to care
for them. Finally the folks said we would have to
get rid of them, and we were compensated with the
money they brought at the market. Two by two
we boxed them up and said good-bye, keeping back
the tears only by thoughts of the fifty cents that
would be ours at the end of market day.

Sometimes I went to the market with mother and
grandfather. I liked to go and think I was of some
little service to them—besides just being company.
Papertown was not a large place but it had four big
paper mills. It was very interesting to go through
them and watch all sorts of filthy-looking rags being made into nice, white paper and folded away
in bundles.

The rag room was of special interest to me. Here
the buttons were cut from the old clothing and sold
for ten cents a quart. There was a large variety and
I amused myself many a rainy day sorting the buttons mother bought and sewing them properly on
cards, like new ones. I think that even now, after
twenty years, mother has some of those very buttons, and I do not believe that she has bought many
in between. Somehow these always seemed to fill any
need.

I liked the Harrisburg market, too. It was very
different from Papertown. In Harrisburg we had a
stall and went to the same spot each time; in Papertown we drove about and sold our goods from door
to door. The eighteen mile drive to Harrisburg often
grew very monotonous until the old Susquehanna

came into sight. The long bridge across it was entirely covered and divided into two parts by a huge partition—so all the wagons going in the same direction were on one side. This bridge was noted for its holdups, especially of the marketmen going home after disposing of their goods. These holdups sounded very exciting to us but we never met with any trouble.

The little country fields in Pennsylvania, with their lanes and meadows dotted with cattle and sheep here and there, are very picturesque. I remember the charm of bringing home the cows and sheep in the evening; sauntering by the rill in the meadow; opening and shutting the bars; watching the water wheel while the cattle stopped to drink by the little waterfall that made it go round; the weathercock on the barn; the windmill that marked the corner of the washhouse roof and showed the handiwork of the boys; the foot-log, which really was a log, that crossed the little stream edged with blue forget-me-nots as far as the eye could carry; the water gate under the log; the weeping willows that came together overhead and shut out the glare of the sunshine as well as the blue of the sky; and the pretty dandelions, like stars that lived in the grass by day and hung in the heavens at night. All these bring to my mind an ideal picture of many a summer evening.

When I read stories of sheep washing and sheep-shearing and hunting for the lost sheep, I do not have to imagine it at all, for I have seen it all, many

times. But I do not like to think much about the
sheep. They are such innocent little things and one
loves them so. True, it is for their wool that we
keep them and it must be taken away from them
somehow, both for our sake and for their own, too;
but often the shearers were careless and cut great
gashes in the sheep. Sometimes the poor things were
sore and lame for days together. It used to make me
cry and was the one horror of the otherwise interesting occasion of sheepshearing.

Perhaps I am writing too much about the things
which pleased me in those days, and too little about
the less pleasant things. Mamma worked cheerfully
and willingly for us, but I heard her sighing sometimes and wishing she had her little family to herself.

Her greatest trial was dear Uncle Rell who had
thick black curly hair and was a very independent
young man who liked to drive a fast horse and sport
the girls around and boss everything generally. He
made us children toe the mark when he was in sight.
And he had no scruples as to whose feelings were
hurt if anyone stood in the way of his doing as he
pleased.

He always wanted to look nice when he went
calling, but mamma was not an expert at ironing
and sometimes she would not get his shirts done
well enough to suit him. More than once I have seen
him come downstairs on a Sunday morning and
crumple up a clean shirt and throw it in her face
with some mean, hateful remark. Mamma would

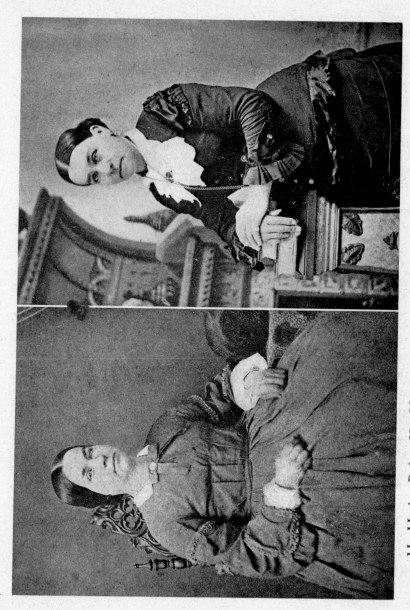

My Mother Before Her Marriage   My Mother Upon Her Arrival in Kansas in
1878

pick it up and put it in with the dirty clothes and go on with her work, crying. Of course if she had said anything, we could not have stayed and she knew it, but those little things, which were cruel and thoughtless, were the only really unpleasant things.

During the four years we were at grandmother's we kept quite well. Once, soon after we had gone there, little Noble "took an ailing spell," and no one could seem to decide what was wrong with him. Finally it was suggested that he was homesick for the place in which he was born. So, one day grandmother took him and me in the buggy and we went back to the old home in Adams County. The people who lived in the house there were strangers to us, but grandmother told them about the baby, and how she thought he was just homesick to come back to this place.

The lady who lived there then was very kind and cordial and gave us our dinner. We stayed all day. Grandmother let Noble creep (he could not walk) all about the place, upstairs and down and out of doors into the yard. Later in the afternoon he cried for his mother. Then grandmother took off his shoes, put a little fine dirt in them and put them on his feet again. This was supposed to be a cure for homesickness. Then we went home. He seemed to be all right afterward and the folks said he was cured.

When Noble was about two years old he had "white swelling" in one of his knees. For sometime the knee was quite stiff, and the doctor said it might always remain so. Fortunately he was mistaken, for Noble outgrew it entirely.

One day when I was helping mother with the washing, I had an accident of my own making. I was turning the washing machine with my right hand, and I kept feeding some shavings into the cogwheels to see them get fluted. I caught my front finger, cutting it off just at the top of the nail. It left a scar and a finger not quite long enough. Grandmother tied up the ragged cut with real sympathy, and my mother excused me from helping with the washing any more that day. When suppertime came and my bandaged finger was explained, grandfather said, "We usually get what we fish for. Your business was turning the washing machine." And Uncle Rell said, "It will teach you to do one thing at a time." But it didn't.

Mother was always remarkably ruddy and healthy. Through all her years in the East, she complained only once during the third year of our stay with the grandparents. She was taken quite suddenly with pains that made her almost frantic. She was ready to scream when we looked at her and was obliged to go to bed almost immediately.

The ailment proved to be inflammatory rheumatism and she was in bed for sixteen weeks. I can remember how she cried with pain, and how the doctors (for a long time two of them came together) used to cup her, using some sort of square instrument at various places on the body. When they took

it off, it was full of blood and left a number of little
cuts where it had been.

I remember coming into mother's room one day
after her session with the physicians. Mother was
showing grandmother her hip. I was not supposed
to see it but I did and immediately remarked that
it "looked like a crazy quilt," whereupon mother
said that she thought it was at least a crazy thing
they were doing, for it did not seem to make her
any better and she always dreaded the ordeal. After
that siege, she was never bedfast again, although I
am sure she has complained of being stiff after many
a hard job of work in Kansas.

Chapter 9

W E had been at grandfather's a little more than
four years when he said one day that it broke
his heart to complain and to suggest that some other
disposition be made in regard to our future, but he
felt he must. He was getting old, and as the children
were getting bigger each day, it cost a great deal to
keep them. For these and other reasons he felt it was
due to him that we be "bound out" to some of the
kind friends who wanted to take a little orphan to
bring up. (We would call this adopting a child.)

This was too much for mother. She said it must
not, could not, be.

Just one year before, a friend by the name of
Jackson Coulson had left the home folks and gone
far out west to Kansas; every little while a letter
had come from him, with glowing descriptions of
the wonderful country and its possibilities for the
future to the man who had little or nothing. Uncle
Amos, who had never made much of a success of
his trade as a tanner, was quite ready to change his
business if anything of any promise came his way,
and Jackson's letters pleased him. When mother
faced separation from us, she wrote to Jackson. He
urged her to come West and bring her family. So

she talked to Amos and the two agreed that Amos should make the trip and see with his own eyes how things were. Mother promised to bear half his expenses out of money paid to her every week which she managed to keep for her use. We children were clothed and fed by grandfather and she saved every penny.

When the new year (1878) opened, Amos was on his way to Kansas. He stayed about a month and came home with the western fever sure enough. He was absolutely *sure* it was the place for his own and mother's family to grow up. Immediately, great plans were set afoot to make ready for the proposed change. Mother had very little money left. During the years she had paid the $300 debt left by father's death, and had accumulated savings from the sale of our garden truck, amounting to about $300. By the time Uncle Amos paid his debts after disposing of all his goods, he would have about the same amount, and to leave home and face an uncertain future with two such families as his and mother's on $600 required a great deal of courage.

But the decision was made. They would go. At once a grand rush began for they must be off as soon as possible, so they could put in a spring crop. Bills were printed and posted over the country announcing a clean-up sale of all the belongings of Amos Heikes and Amanda Knisely on February 14. The day came—a cold, half-snowing-half-raining day—when everything was unpleasant and everybody felt cross and uncomfortable. But it was a busy day for us, and by the time night came and the lights were lit, there was no home and no nothing. All our possessions were scattered far and wide. During the two weeks that followed, Uncle Amos's family visited among friends. Immediately after the sale, such things as had been kept out to take to Kansas were packed, crated, taken to town and started on their way to the West, with the hope that they might arrive ahead of the families and be ready for use when they got there. All our friends for miles around came to say good-bye, and to express their approval or disapproval, to cry or be dignified as their natures dictated. As I remember it, most of them were about as helpful as the average comforter after a funeral. I used to feel so keenly those days that there were many occasions when silence would have been much kinder than words. We were *going* —and what was there to be said about it?

I went around among all my friends to spend a night and say good-bye, and I knew it would be hard to come away and leave them. Mother had set about doing all sorts of things. Each of the boys was to have a new suit. She made them out of dark-colored homespun, too big by two or three sizes, but you see they would have to *last*. Then she bought a bolt of flannel. She still has some of the garments made from that red and black checked goods—there was no wear-out to it. There were also a few new blankets and some new dresses. It was a strange outfit that she got together. On the whole it was a very good one, though she made some mistakes and brought a few useless things with her.

Two weeks before we were to start, half the children took down with measles. The well ones were kept with the sick ones so they would take them too and have it over with. My little sister Leah was the only one who persisted in keeping well. We were to start on Monday, March 4. On the afternoon of the third, the trunks were sent to town. The tickets were bought and in Uncle Amos's pocket. There was nothing more to do but to put the lunch into the satchels and be off to the train, which left at ten o'clock in the morning. That night about midnight, Leah awakened mother with her crying and said, "I'm in such a fix," and by morning she was red with measles. She was pretty sick, too, but no one entertained any doubt as to what was to be done. She was wrapped in a big shawl and we started. We would not think of taking such chances now, and it is too bad we did then, for there is no telling how many people suffered from the foolish deed. As far as Leah was concerned, however, when we landed in Kansas on Thursday evening, March 7, 1878, she was quite herself.

We left grandfather's on Monday morning, March 4, 1878, for the little town of Dillsburg, three miles away, and I think the older members of the party waved hands and cried all the way to town. The homes were close together, and all the people along the road knew we were leaving so we could not help being a little tearful. Both grandparents were with us, as well as Uncle Rell. We were all ready to board the train and did not have long to wait for its coming. Soon we were settled and off for a long journey. It was rather gloomy until we passed through all the territory familiar to the grown folks, and then it began to be a bit more interesting to them and a lot more cheerful for the children. We looked forward to a long, hard monotonous ride, but it really was not as bad as we had feared.

In our party were Uncle Amos and his wife, Aunt Leah, with their six children; Cousin Loll (cousin to Uncle Amos and mother), and his wife Ellen (sister to Aunt Leah), newly married and going West to try their fortunes; Milt Howard, a young man coming to Kansas to assist an uncle who had settled near Abilene some years before; and mother and her six children. I was the oldest of the twelve children in the party and approaching my fifteenth birthday in April. Everyone who was big enough to do so carried a bundle, and we must have looked like immigrants "just over." Wouldn't a picture of us as we looked that day be funny now? I could not begin to tell the things we carried, but we had the usual bandbox, some old-fashioned carpetbags, and some shawl straps and bundles that could not be described. The bandbox was the biggest nuisance of all. In the first place, it was always in the way, and about to be crushed. Things had been packed into every nook and corner, and in the hurry and rush of it all, some things were forgotten. Grandmother had packed some rolls in the bandbox, putting them in the crown of the hat that was on the bottom. Before we got to Kansas, the box sprang a leak and crumbs from these slipped through the opening. It was not until we undid the bandbox, days after getting there, that we found out what had kept things messed up.

We traveled over what was known as the Panhandle Route, through St. Louis, Kansas City, and Topeka to Abilene. Just a few things are clear in my mind concerning the journey itself. At Harrisburg we were anxious to have one last look at the old wagon bridge we had crossed so many times. The city of Altoona stands out clearly in my memory as a very dirty-looking place, and to this day I have never seen its grimy, black look surpassed. Horseshoe Bend, at Pittsburgh, was most interesting, and we were all able to get a good look before it was lost to view. Because it was so early in the spring, things were not green, but there was promise everywhere, and the farther west we came the nearer spring seemed to be. I recall only the names of Columbus and Indianapolis, but when we got to St. Louis we had a few hours to wait before leaving for Kansas City. We had not been out of our car before this, and it was a wonderful relief to have a little chance to stretch our legs and work off a bit of surplus energy. (Our childish energy was nigh to being the death of the older people sometimes.) Although some of the crowd suffered from car sickness to a greater or less degree, as a whole it was a pretty lively bunch. We took in the entire station, and realized it was more wonderful than anything we had ever seen, but the mere fact of getting outside that car was the real treat. The older members of the party said they were glad when it was time to go, but some of us could not understand this. We were having such an awfully good time.

We traveled on what was known as an immigrant train. The seats had straw coverings just as they have now (1899) but the car was not a sleeper. We had to sit up all the way or lie down on somebody else or on some of the baggage. I remember the crowding. It seemed as if we were packing and unpacking and moving something all the time. We brought all our lunch with us for the entire trip, and it meant something to arrange that much food, to say nothing of anything else. Then when one considers that two of the children were babes in arms and that at least half of the twelve had not yet learned to spread their own bread with butter and that Leah had the measles and needed special care, one realizes that there must have been some discomfort. Matters were made harder, too, by the fact that six of the children rode free and three on half fare, and that meant fewer seats than there should have been for so large a company. The train was loaded with people going to various parts of the west, and there were other families on the train with just as many little children as we had. Some of them were howling all the time or making noise of some sort. I think we ate through most of the waking hours.

One of the women was continually fixing something for someone to eat and we would walk to her seat, get something in our hand and go back to our seat to eat it. I cannot see how we got through the nights and days of that long journey, but like most things it came to an end finally.

We arrived in Abilene at five o'clock in the evening, March 7, 1878, after seventy-nine hours sitting in almost the same spot, tired, worn out and desperately homesick. When we got off the train the wind was blowing a perfect March gale around that old depot, and the first thing we knew half the children were running after their hats which were flying in every direction. The folks had expected their friend Mr. Coulson to meet us, but he was not on hand. They hardly knew what to do, but concluded that any arrangement to get out of town would be cheaper and better than staying there. In central Kansas March days are not very long, but the older members of the party went uptown to look around; the men for a way to get out, the women for a stove and such other things as they would need to do the housekeeping. I was left at the depot with the twelve children.

When the folks came back, after what seemed hours to me, some of the children were crying, some of them were lying on the floor, fast asleep, while the older ones were wandering about, doing the best they could to be brave and helpful.

While the men had been trying to find someone to drive us out to the country, they had met an old friend, a man named Livingston, who had come West some years before. He lived about ten miles north of town and had come in for supplies; he was just starting for home. When Amos and Loll told him of the situation we were in, he agreed to store his load of goods in town and return for it next day, so he could do something for us. The plan was to go directly to Jackson Coulson's, and I think that further than that no one knew just what we would do. The Coulsons lived twenty miles north of Abilene. Mr. Livingston had a light Studebaker wagon drawn by two little Texas ponies. There were eighteen of us and Mr. Livingston, plus all our satchels, bags and bundles. It was impossible to put everybody and everything in the wagon at once, and even if it could have been done, the ponies could not have pulled the load. It was decided to load the baggage and the babies. The rest of us walked, except for short turns, in the wagon by relays, when we got too tired to go on. Of course, we made very slow progress, but we kept on hour after hour through the night.

That night was a memorable one for there were no well-defined roads across the prairie. Our driver had never been so far north and he was not quite sure that he could take us to the right place. The moon was shining brightly, and this was a joy and satisfaction. All about us on every side was nothing but unbroken prairie. There was not a sign of a tree nor a foot of fence. Once in a long distance there was a house or shelter for some immigrant who had dared to try his fortune on the "Great American Desert." There was nothing to break the monotony save prairie fires and the howl of the wolves. Now and then jack rabbits would jump up and run away, and we thought that they were extraordinary examples of rabbits. They ran very fast and looked as big as dogs in the moonlight, we thought. We learned to know them better, much better, in later days.

Several times prairie chickens in twos and threes or in flocks were disturbed by our coming and flew across our path. We could form but a vague idea of what they really were, for they looked so much like the night. We realized only that they were big birds that made a noise. But there were days ahead when they were to play a great part in our lives. We ate their flesh and hunted their eggs—a great help when there was so little to fill so many hungry mouths.

The "ride" was monotonous because we were so tired and so cramped and there was no variety in the scene. And yet, I have never taken a trip in my life that was more exciting than that one. In the first place, the relay plan of walking and riding was new and different and very hard. The silence of God's great out-of-doors in the nighttime was awe inspiring. The blue sky, so very blue, dotted with many stars, and a moon as bright as a moon could be, were the subjects of much conversation. It was comforting to us to think that we saw the same moon that was shining over the folks in old Pennsylvania, and to know they were thinking of us.

Until half the distance had been covered and all those had gone to sleep who could dispose their bodies to do so, there was one exclamation after another about the prairie fires. There were many of them and we could not understand why fires should be running wild like that. We were told that people were burning off the dead grass to make better grass in the summer. These fires were dangerous, but there were so few people around that there was seldom any damage. As people began to settle the country more and more, nothing was more feared as a menace to property and lives than these prairie fires. As soon as a house was built, a firebreak was made. This was done by plowing a circle around the house, some feet away. The swath was from ten to twenty feet wide. Not a stack of hay was put up without making a break about it and no machinery was left on the grass. Yet in spite of all these precautions sometimes a fire would get out of hand, and if a hard wind was blowing, then there would be much excitement. I have seen the folks in Dickinson County work until they were exhausted, fighting to keep the fire from burning up their homes or their grain and haystacks. They built a fire in front of the fire path and that was usually the most effective way to fight it but sometimes nothing helped. Bits of flaming material would leap over and ignite the grass in a dozen spots—just as if one were to throw out a bunch of lighted firecrackers. We kept sacks and

wire on hand to tie to forks and shovels and anything we could get, and those were used to beat out
the fire. It was desperately hard work, but had to
be done. Even at that many and many a family lost
everything they had in those early-day prairie fires.
When I read of the forest fires in the North now,
I always think of the times when we tusseled with
prairie fires and dreaded them.

It was two o'clock in the morning when we
stopped in front of Mr. Coulson's little prairie
house. In the moonlight no sign of life was visible
and outside of the house there was nothing but a
straw pile. How lonely and wild it all seemed and
how the wind did blow around that house! As we
waited outside for an answer to our rather boister-
ous hallo, I thought of a good many things. How
was it ever going to be possible to stop at such a little
house—not even as large as the old washhouse at
home, nor half so inviting as the tent on the camp-
ground? Surely we could not stop here. And how in
the world could *six* people live in such a place?

After what seemed a long time, but in reality was
only a few minutes, the door opened and there stood
Jackson. As soon as the situation could be made
clear to him, we received a cordial welcome. Jane,
his wife, was on hand before we were unloaded, and
soon we were all *piled*, yes, literally *piled*, into the
house; in fact, into one tiny room. The Coulsons
had not received our letter telling that we were coming, so our arrival was a complete surprise. It made

a rather queer situation all around for there were six of them and nineteen of us.

The house was one and a half stories high, twenty feet long and eighteen feet wide. There were two windows and a door downstairs. It was unplastered and unpainted, both inside and out. There was a loft, and the floor on each side touched the eaves of the roof. There was no outside opening to the loft; it was reached by a ladder that extended through a hole in the ceiling in one corner of the room.

While the men went to the barn with the ponies, Jane built a fire in the little cookstove. This she did by filling it with ears of corn, pouring on kerosene and throwing in a lighted match. I thought we would be burned up sure enough, and the extravagance of burning *corn* was most shocking. She did not seem to notice my discomfiture, but filled the coffee pot and put it and the teakettle on the stove; then she took a pan and put some flour into it. In a little while she had some nice soda biscuits and hot coffee on the table and told us to help ourselves. There was no butter, no jelly—just biscuits and coffee and a little milk. I had never seen such poverty in all my life. I certainly hoped we would not have to have a table like that. I could not eat a bite.

I was homesick already and wished we had stayed in the East even if we had to live with strange people. Anything would have been better than this. Where and how could we possibly sleep? It was all we could do to stand up. There were only two chairs, a bench, a rude table, a cupboard and cookstove in the room. Hanging on nails in the uprights on one side was a little clothing. To me everything looked like desolation itself.

After all who wanted it had taken refreshment, Jane and Jackson, for so the folks addressed the Coulsons, climbed up the ladder to the loft overhead. A child was handed up to them, then another, and so on until all got upstairs to sleep. Our baggage and all the bedding the little house afforded was spread out over the board floor, and we were laid side by side, with our feet toward the eaves and our heads toward the center, leaving a path right down the middle. Even in the center the grown folks could not stand erect, and there was no room for undressing anywhere. I cannot see how we rested at all. We were completely worn out, and we were wearing the same clothing we had left home in Monday morning. But one can do a world of things he would not dream of doing unless circumstances demand it.

When we had all stretched out on the floor two men lay down near the ladder hole so none of the children would fall through. Then the furniture downstairs was put outside the house and in that room those who could not get upstairs were free to make themselves as comfortable as they could. In spite of the seeming discomfiture we slept, some of us, quite late into the next day. *Twenty-five people* in this way cuddled into that little house that night for shelter.

With my waking moments, the longing for home

and comfort returned to me, and when I climbed
down the ladder I was ready to break into tears.
Jane greeted me with the dreadful news that all the
grown folks had gone—some back to Abilene with
Mr. Livingston and others across country to find a
place for us to stay. I was to take good care of the
children. By that time I felt I surely had something
to cry about for I did want to see mother. However,
the children were beginning to awaken and I was
busy enough for a while trying to wash them and
comb their hair, and that kept me from my thoughts
a little while. Jane made some breakfast and we fed
as many children at a time as we could. The table
would not hold more than six, and because there
were only four seats and we could handle more
standing, most of us stood up to eat.

The Coulsons had a good cow, and the smaller
children had milk to drink, but the older ones had
only biscuits and milk gravy made with lard. That
was all Jane had to give us and all she had for herself and family. We learned to be glad and thankful
for that much. Cornmeal mush furnished a little
variety. We ate that fried or with milk. Jane made
what butter she could but there was very little
cream. A few dozen chickens provided some eggs
which helped out. Bacon was the only indulgence.
It happened that we got there just as the butter ran
out and there was not cream enough to churn more.
A hen had been set the day before and not an egg
was on hand. The bacon, too, had been cleaned to
the rind. Jackson had meant to get some when he

went to town, but he had been busy and had not gone for provisions.

Flour, corn meal, lard and milk! It seemed nothing at all, and we were *so* hungry. We had had no cooked food for four whole days. I have realized since, however, how remarkable it was that Jane could do so many different things with those few supplies. We were there for three days and nights and in the days that followed we learned how to get along with very little and to be happy, too.

Those first days were very trying indeed. When we opened the door we were greeted by a wind so strong that we had to hold fast to the doorknob to keep from being blown from the little stone step. Our hats twisted around on our heads and our clothing whipped about wildly in the wind. The view was truly wonderful, but I could see nothing, nothing, nothing. As far as the eye carried there was no house, no fence, no tree—only undulating stretches of prairie with here and there a little patch of plowed ground or a spot of green. I thought it was a desert.

The little unpainted house in which we were staying had no porch. The washtub stood under the eaves to catch a bit of soft water, should it ever rain—and I wondered if it ever did rain, or if the wind just blew all the time. Not far away was a big pile of straw; this sheltered the ox team and the cow at night. An empty wagon and plow stood nearby. Here and there chickens were scratching in the straw or the little pile of corn that lay on the ground. A little black pig squealed in a pen made of stones and sticks and I wondered if it was hungry too, as I was. Between the house and the straw barn was a bored well; and not another thing could I see but brown grass and blue sky to the north and south and to the east and to the west. It was a depressing picture.

The wind was too cool as well as too strong for us to let the smaller children out-of-doors, so they all crowded inside. To help complicate matters, Howard went too near one of the oxen and it kicked him on the leg; and with both a sore leg and an empty stomach he found something to cry about all day. When night came, we longed for the folks to come home but finally we had to go to bed without seeing them. Youth sleeps soundly and easily and does not waste the night in worry—which is truly a wonderful provision of our Heavenly Father. We slept well and long and the sun was high in the sky when I opened my eyes next morning. Not a sound could I hear, but I was down the ladder looking for someone in almost no time. The kitchen or dining room, or whatever it was, was empty. I went to the straw barn and saw Jane working around, but no one else. I asked for mother and her answer almost sickened me; there were so many things to do that the folks had gone right back early in the morning to finish up their business in town.

Perhaps it was because I was heavy hearted that my job seemed so hard that day, but whatever the reason, the children were harder to get along with.

The little ones seemed restless, the middle-sized ones cried loudly for their mothers and the bigger ones would not mind. I thought that Jane was too harsh with me, but when I think of it now, I wonder how she endured those three days, when all that mob descended on her quiet little home like a cyclone. It would have been bad enough had the mothers been on hand to look after the children, but twelve children were left with a mother who had four of her own, all under seven years of age. Only two of us were old enough to help—I was fourteen and Annie, Uncle Amos's eldest, was twelve. This brought the total up to sixteen children under fifteen years of age, in a room eighteen by twenty feet, where all the cooking and eating and bathing and combing and cleaning had to be done—my head swims now as I recall the scene. Our folks asked a lot of these friends. I wondered how they could ever remain friends afterward, but they did. The families have visited back and forth through all the years since.

With the exception of Milt Howard, who returned to his own people with Mr. Livingston, we all stayed on with these kind people until the folks succeeded in finding a dwelling place and getting it ready for us. On the evening of the third day, with the baggage which we had brought with us, the freight which had arrived in Abilene, and the new purchases made in the town, we moved to a place a mile and a half south of Mr. Coulson's.

The house was a mere shell, fourteen by twenty

feet, and was not plastered. There was a door and window on either side, a chimney at the north end, and only rafters and roof overhead. We had brought with us from Pennsylvania two bedsteads and a cot. The beds did not have slats, but ropes woven back and forth and fastened to little pegs served that purpose. On these ropes we laid our bedticks. We had no mattresses.

The two beds were put up with footends together, and they just reached across the room at one end. Over the top of the two beds a berth was built from lumber brought from town. Straw was spread on this and then covered over with the bedding we had; and here ten of us piled up each night to sleep. Loll and Ellen occupied one of the beds—Uncle Amos and his wife and baby the other—mother and one of the smaller children slept on the cot. We had bought a new cookstove in town, but no table, so we ate off of one of the boxes that had held some of the freight. This stood in the middle of the room, and when we ate our meals we had a sort of cafeteria without knowing it. We all took what we wanted and then those who could find boxes or a place on the edge of the bed, took seats and ate. The rest of us stood or sat on the floor.

Aunt Leah and Cousin Ella did the cooking and the housekeeping, such as it was. Mother went about planning and working with Uncle Amos and Loll. We fared much better for something to eat here than at the home of our friends because we had brought a good many eatables with us and decided we might as well use them at one time as another. Besides we really had no place to preserve them.

This little house was an abandoned one out in the middle of nowhere. Someone had tried to dig a well but was not successful, so all our water had to be carried more than half a mile. Some days the wind was so strong that it would blow half the water out of the bucket before we could get it home, and the half that was left was so dirty no one wanted to drink any of it. Washing under such conditions must have been a nightmare. The clothing was taken away from home, washed, then carried back and dried on the grass.

There was no fuel to burn but corn and that cost fifteen cents a bushel.

We had lived together in this fashion for a week, when a neighbor half a mile away—at the place where we got our water—said she would plan somehow to give mother's family a room in which to sleep. That was a great relief. Mother at once took her bedding and her family and we moved into the room so kindly offered, but we kept on taking our meals in the little house with our own folks. A week later we rented eighty acres next to the Hursh's, where we had our room. There was a little log house twelve by twelve with just four walls and a roof. The spaces between the logs looked as if they had been filled with wet mud.

Into this little house, mother moved her family, though of course, seven people could not *live* in so small a space. With the stove and box table and a few trunks, it was full. There was a good straw stable not far from the house, and mother at once decided that we would use that for our sleeping quarters. It was fresh and clean, in contrast to the house, which we found infested with bedbugs. Mother thought it was a good providence that had prevented putting our bedding into the house.

All went well for some nights and we congratulated ourselves on having such a comfortable place to sleep. We had not thought of being afraid, for surely there was nothing around that could possibly hurt us. One night mother and I were awakened at the same time by something moving about in the straw. At one end of the stable mangers had been built in to feed the cattle, and it was across the top of these that we had made our beds. The front of the bed was above the ground, and the back of it was close against the straw cover of the barn. It was very dark, and there was at no time any possibility of a light at night in that place, so for some moments we lay in great suspense. We got up and were growing thoroughly frightened, when a familiar grunt told us what had invaded our sleeping apartment. The next thing was how to get the animal out. It was pitch dark, and we could not tell where we were or what we were about. However, after much yelling and running to and fro, and after the hog, which weighed about a hundred and fifty pounds, had run over almost every one of us, it went out through the door. The hog belonging to our neighbor, Hursh, had come to the straw stack to hunt for loose wheat. It climbed up on the side, and fell through the thatch into the stable and onto one of the beds. We always wondered how it happened that no one was hurt in this scuffle.

This ended sleeping in the barn for mother. She would have no more of it. We had brought a little ten-by-twelve soldier tent with us and this we set up at the front of the house, with the opening close to the door. Uncle Amos put up some bunks for us and there we slept for the remaining month. A day or two before we left that place mother awoke in the morning and thought she saw something crawling on the ground. She was startled sure enough, for it was a little snake, and it wiggled off under one of the beds. Mother was very ill at ease when the night-time came, and I think often went to bed fearing and wondering "What next?"

The first step toward the farming was the purchase of a yoke of nice red oxen, of good size and quite amiable, for putting out some spring wheat. We named the oxen Jim and Dick and drove them to the wagon as well as the plow. Loll immediately went to work on the eighty acres. All the women-folks and Amos dug up the ground and made a big garden, and things came up nicely and promised to yield well. A few weeks later mother and Amos found the farm on which mother lives now in north Dickinson county. It was a piece of railroad land and the purchase price was $5.50 an acre. Only a little was to be paid down and they hoped the rest of the payments would not be hard to meet.

After moving into the little log house, mother had bought a red cow and her little red calf. We called the mother Curly because she had a crumpled horn. We kept her for many years. We had been getting along all this time without any butter for our bread and missed it very much, but did not have enough cream to make churning worth while. On the day when it seemed we might have enough cream, mother, for some reason, had to go away. She said I should churn the butter, that I was plenty big enough and she was sure I knew how. In fact, she told me *just* how, the last thing before she left home.

We had brought a new churn with us from the East. It had not been used before, and I was in such a hurry to make the cream into butter that I never stopped to look into the churn. I poured in the cream and began to turn the crank. I was so glad when I felt it growing thicker that I danced up and down in my joy at the thought of the good buttered bread we would have.

Oh! Oh! Oh! You could never imagine my feelings when I opened that churn! I had yellow butter all right, but I also had chips and shavings, and they were all mixed up with the butter. It had to be thrown away—and there we were, desperately hungry for it. Mother scolded me and hoped I had learned a lesson, but that part of it did not matter at all—nothing mattered except the tragic loss of that long anticipated butter.

Soon another yoke of oxen was purchased—

white, this time—so we could plow up more new ground. Plowing was pretty hard work, but we were happy to do it, and all of us took a turn at it. Sometimes the oxen would run away from us in spite of all we could do; we had some narrow escapes, but were never hurt. When the oxen wanted a drink of water, they would start for the creek a quarter of a mile away, and all we could do was to turn the plow on edge and follow. After that, it was no trouble to drive them back to work again. They would do the same thing when they were hitched to the wagon if they were thirsty. Occasionally they ran down steep banks and damaged the wagon. The boys were especially fond of Dick because they could ride him. None of the other three oxen permitted such liberties. I tried riding him once, but he threw me off, kicked me and tore my dress. I never tried it the second time. We sometimes used the oxen to bring large loads from Abilene, starting at eleven or twelve o'clock at night and getting to town—fifteen miles away—at perhaps eight or nine o'clock. If we were able to leave town by noon, we got home at midnight or later. It surely was a sore trial to drive thirty miles with a team of oxen, but that's what we had to do.

We did not have fenced pastures into which we could turn our oxen, when we were through with the day's work nor did we have grain to feed them. There were no trees nor posts to tie them to in those days, so we had to picket them some place where they might eat in the night. We put a rope around their big horns, and to this we fastened another rope by means of a swivel—a little iron arrangement that kept the rope from twisting up on itself. We made it as long or short as necessary and fastened it to an iron stake to which another swivel was attached. When we found a nice place for the ox or cow to eat, we would drive the stake into the ground. This was never an easy job, for it came in the evening when we were dead tired anyway, and when the animals wanted to do anything but what we wanted them to do, so things could get pretty desperate. Howard, Dave and I, always had to put out the oxen when we finished plowing at night. We did most of our plowing in our bare feet, for we wore shoes out very quickly, and there was little money for buying new ones. One evening I was taking the two white oxen down across the little ravine beyond the creek. They were tied with a rope which I held in my hand, together with my stake. They were in such a hurry to get to the creek that I was dragged along after them helplessly. I tried to drop my stakes, but my hands had caught in the rope and I could not let go of anything. In my vain effort to try to keep up with them and keep on my feet at the same time, I lost my balance and fell. It was not very far to the water but far enough to tear off my clothing and bruise my hips and shoulders. As soon as they stopped, I worked myself loose and stretched out my arms, and then a queer reaction came to me —I forgot all my hurts in a fit of anger and called those dumb beasts all kinds of names. By that time

they finished drinking, raised their heads, looked
peacefully about as if to say thank you, and lifting
their clumsy bodies step by step to the creek bank,
they walked over to a green spot and began to graze.
I picked up my stakes, hammered them into the
ground and dragged painfully up the hill to the
house, feeling ashamed of myself every step of the
way and wondering why people get angry and in-
jure themselves.

Our work, as I think of it now, may have been
monotonous, but I am sure it did not seem so to us
then. We had a great object in view, and we imagined all sorts of fine results for our labor. The prairie
chickens were plentiful—Loll used to shoot them by
the dozen. They were good to eat, and helped out
a lot when there was no money to buy the food
we might have liked better. They made their nests in
the open and we have found as many as twenty eggs
in one nest. Dave and Elmer would often go along
and look for eggs while we plowed.

There were lots of snakes, too. They made their
nests just far enough under the sod for the plow
to cut the nest in two, and it was not at all uncommon to turn out a great bunch of them. We had to
jump to hold onto the plow and get over without
stepping into them. I never got to the place where
I could cross a nest of snakes and keep calm in mind.
Dave became expert at catching them by the tail,
giving them a jerk and cracking off their heads. One
day, we saw a big bull snake, and as it made for its
hole, Dave went after it. It had started down the

hole, but when Dave arrived there was enough of its tail outside for him to grasp. He pulled and pulled and finally Mr. Snake let go all at once. Dave fell backward with the snake on top of him, but he did not let go. I screamed and yelled, I do not know why, because there was nothing for him to do but fight it out, and he did. Mother hoped he might stop if he had a good scare, but he continued to crack every snake he could catch.

That spring Howard, Dave and I broke eighty acres of the new ground. Breaking sod is not like ordinary plowing. In the first place, the plow itself is different. The end must be very sharp to cut all the roots, and this share had to be sharpened often. Then there is a sharp wheel that cuts a line, marking the width of ground to be turned over by the plow. When the prairie sod was first turned it was very tough and nothing was done with it until it rotted. So, although we had all the ground we wanted—one hundred and sixty acres—we had no place to do any planting. But we just had to plant *something*. So we cut holes in the sod with a hatchet and dropped seeds into them—citron, melons of all kinds, pumpkins and corn. With the exception of the corn we have never, in any year since, had such returns. There were loads of everything. The melons were wonderful. We supplied the country for miles around and enjoyed plenty of them ourselves. Mother used to say it was the easiest thing she ever did in her life. No hoeing, no bugs to fight, nothing to do but gather the fruit.

In the fall a drill was hired and eighty acres were
sown in wheat.

Meanwhile, through the summer months the
house was slowly being built, and late in the fall
Uncle Amos brought down his family from the place
to which they had moved in the spring. Everything
was not as lovely as it might have been. In the first
place, Uncle was no carpenter, but he said he could
build the house and he did. It was not a great success nor wholly a failure, for it looked like a house.
On the Fourth of July, while he was building it,
there was a heavy hailstorm and with it a terrifically
high wind. It blew out windows and doors, which
had not been put in permanently, and caused a great
loss and backset to the building. An empty barrel
that stood near the house was blown half a mile,
and parts of the new house were scattered for some
distance over the twenty acres south of the house.
This was our first experience with windstorms, but
not our last.

Uncle did the plastering, too, but he finished it
so late in the fall that it did not get dry before
cold weather. As a result, not a door in the house
would close and we were told we must not cut them
down or they would be altogether too small the
next winter. All these things helped to make a hard
winter harder than it needed to be.

It was very cold all that first winter, with lots of
snow. Money and food were scarce, and we resorted
to everything we could think of to get along. When
we arrived in Abilene, there had not been much

money in the company. Mother had her three hundred dollars and Uncle Amos had less, so it goes without saying that at the end of six months the treasury must have been almost depleted.

Dave and Howard broke sod for a neighbor or two after we finished our field, and that was a help. A family wanted a hired girl, and mother said I must go and do the best I could. I went, and I could not begin to tell the trials of that week. I was a good little helper, I think, but when the woman ordered me to make soda biscuits and pancakes the very first thing—two things always forbidden in our home—I was puzzled, but did the best I could by following directions. Next I was sent to the washtub, but I did not know the first thing about washing, so my employer finally concluded I was no good. She sent me home on half pay—one whole dollar for seven days of torture! I was very much discouraged and felt that I could never go out anywhere as a hired girl again.

Mother decided to keep me at home and to take outside jobs herself. Anything that was asked of her she did—washing, cooking, nursing, butchering, midwifery—anything was in her line if she could earn a little money by it.

I had a second experience working out that summer when a new baby came to a neighbor five or six miles away and they could not get anyone else to help with the work. The man begged mother to come, but she was busy; then he wanted me, and mother urged me to go and do what I could. If he had let me care for the baby I might have done very well, but he did that himself and set me at the house work and the washtub, where I spoiled practically everything I tried to wash. With the kind of care I gave that woman, I wonder that she ever got well. That was another nightmare week in my life.

Chapter 10

ONE of the fine features of the people in the West, in that early day, was their friendly hospitality. Nobody had very much of anything, but what little they had was willingly shared. We did have trouble getting enough to eat the first six months we were in Kansas, but our neighbors, one, two, three and four miles away—Hursh, Miller, Walker and George—gave us potatoes, sauerkraut and other things they had, and so we got along. It was a little hard to be glad after giving up a life of plenty and running over only to come to a place with nothing, absolutely nothing, but grass and blue sky. We could not help longing for the old home back in Pennsylvania. But, after all, that was not our home —for we had no home there any more. Now we were going to have a home—in this big state of Kansas—and so we planned and built our castles in the air, most of which never got any foundations under them.

When I look over the country now with its thousands of beautiful trees and its many pretty homes, I can scarcely make myself believe that I knew it when there was nothing to be seen but the grass and sky. But so it was! The houses then were few and scattered and they were built on hillsides and in hollows to escape the winds and so could not easily be seen. There was not much travel then and we hailed every stranger with delight. The first question was always, "Who are you?" and the next, "Where are you from?" In those days, there was no one old enough to talk who could claim the honor of being born in Kansas.

Buggies were still a curiosity in the West, and I think it was six or eight years before we saw any kind of vehicle drawn by one horse. Two horses or a team of oxen were a necessity because as soon as a road was used for any time, it began to wear down into two paths, side by side. These soon became ruts, and one horse could not have pulled anything over such a road.

We watched most eagerly for the mail. It came to our little post office of Keystone, four miles away, twice each week. Most of the four miles was through rocky hills, known as the Black Hills. One day Annie (Heikes) and I were walking through those hills to get the mail. We had to walk in the ruts of the road. Suddenly we heard the queerest noise we had ever heard. It grew louder, and the first thing we knew we were facing two big rattlesnakes. We cleared the tracks in a hurry and let them go on their way, never stopping to see what became of them. On the way back we went far out of our way on the prairie to miss that part of the road, but those were the only live rattlers I ever saw in Kansas. That same day we saw our first wolves—three of them—and we thought we were having more than our share of adventures all at once. The week before we moved to the Dickinson County farm, someone suggested that perhaps we ought to go to Industry to see if we had any mail there, for we had been writing home that Industry would be our new post office. Annie and I were commissioned to make the trip. It was about five miles and there was a track all the way, so we might have kept in it and been all right. We found Industry, but it seemed a long way. The fact that there was no mail for us made it seem longer, so we decided to cut across the prairie on the homeward trip.

We walked and walked, and it is not at all interesting to walk miles over raw prairie grass and not know where you are going to come out. We finally came to a house where we stopped to rest. The lady was kind, and we told her who we were and all about ourselves, and she, in western fashion, wanted to give us something, so she gave us a big cat which we were foolish to lug along with us. She told us how to go, but it was after dark when we reached home, so tired, so tired. The folks were beginning to get a little anxious about us and feared we might be lost.

It was not an uncommon thing at that time for people to lose themselves on the broad prairies and have to stay out all night. The houses were so far apart and the roads so indistinct, that sometimes it was impossible to find one's way. No one in our family ever got lost, but once when Loll had driven the ox team to Abilene, it grew dark before he got home. He kept on for a little while, but then decided it was too risky, so he picketed the oxen and slept in his wagon all night.

Until a few years before we came to Dickinson County, the whole country had been a Texas cattle range, supporting about 20,000 head. No one took any care of these cattle. Once a year big cattle owners would round them up and pick out their own by the brand. The young cattle were divided among the owners, branded and turned loose to go where they would until time for the next roundup. No attention was paid to them in the winter. There was never any shelter for them, and sometimes in a hard winter they could not get anything to eat. At such times the loss would be appalling.

Just one mile north of our home farm, in a hollow between two hills, there was—and still is—a great pile of bones. Fred George, who lived down on the creek near Industry, had been a cattle boy and had helped round up cattle. He told us that a few years before, some twelve or fifteen hundred cattle had become so cold and hungry that they had crowded together to keep warm. They had either frozen or been crushed to death, and that bone pile was what was left of them. He said the cattle would have spells of stampeding, and then again of huddling together, and in either case nothing could be done to save them.

Fred George was a wonder in my eyes—he knew so much and told such interesting stories. People used to travel by the stars, since there were no paths to follow, and one night after I had my own pony, he and I took a long ride so he could show me how this was done. It was not wholly successful, because now and then our line of travel was spoiled by some new settler and his improvements. Fred was not an educated boy, but he knew a great many things and inspired me with a feeling of awe and confidence. I liked to listen to him.

During the first year, we had neighbors of quite a different sort—two Harvard graduates. We did not get acquainted with them at all, however, and I have often been sorry about this for we failed to get the inspiration they might have given us. These two boys were fine looking, although they were not very strong. They seemed to have plenty of means but they had come out to Kansas to rough it for a year. With only a hammer and saw, they had built a rude house half a mile from us and lived in it all winter. At the end of the year they went back to fine positions as teachers in eastern colleges.

At this time, a Frenchman came into my life. He was leader of a little brass band that met at the schoolhouse just over the way from our home. He was superior to most of the young folks to be found in the country, but he was a great flirt, as at that time I supposed all Frenchmen were. He had considerable ability as a leader, and when he found that mother could sing, he began to call at our house and soon had a singing school organized with mother as the teacher. We met every two weeks.

The young people came from miles around, and much good came from mother's work, which continued through a number of years. The singing class was followed by a Sunday school meeting at the schoolhouse in the afternoon. This was continued until the school building was moved up on the hill, a good many years later.

My French friend was a backer for everything mother tried to do, and he was always very nice to me. I liked him, too, but Uncle Amos began to criticise him and to find fault with mother for allowing me to see so much of him, so I had little encouragement in enjoying his company. Anyway, I learned to know him better than any of the other boys. But when I went away to school I had to forget about boys.

When our house was finished it was one of the best as well as the largest in that part of the country. The George family had also moved into a new house, built of stone. They had lived in a dugout for several years, and they told us many queer things about it. We knew the old sod house well. It was used later as a sort of storehouse. The four sides were made of sod piled layer upon layer. The door was at one end. The roof was made of long limbs, brought from trees growing on the creek banks, stretching from side to side. On these were brush and sod, covered with dirt and gravel. After every rain it had to be repaired.

The whole thing made an ideal place for all kinds of animals to find a home. It was warm and inviting and they came. Fred told us how one day when they were eating dinner they had a startling surprise. The soup, which was their dinner that day, was set in the middle of the table. They had just been seated and were about to dish out the soup with a big dipper, when *kersplash!* something went into the soup, and the dipper his mother was holding went to the bottom in a hurry. Before they could jump from their seats, the big snake—for that was their uninvited guest—raised its head out of the soup, crawled over the top of the kettle onto the table, dropped to the floor and made for the door. John found words first and said, "It's nothing but a bull snake," and catching it by the tail, he took it outside and sent its head flying.

These snakes were not dangerous, but there were a good many of them, and they made us creepy sometimes. When I taught my first term of school, a family who lived in a dugout waked one morning to find a three-foot snake in bed with them, dead. They concluded it had fallen from its hiding place among the branches in the roof and that they had rolled on it and killed it while they slept.

When we first came to Kansas, the climate was nothing like it is today. The winds then were not hot as they are now, but they blew incessantly and so powerfully that one could scarcely walk against them. It was worse in the daytime than at night. It seldom rained in the daytime, and the night showers were nearly always local and sometimes covered very small areas. After five or six years, all this began to change. Planting trees and tilling the soil made a difference. When a man started his home, he planted trees, and it was not long before we recognized the occupied quarter section by the clump of trees that was sure to be there. Sometimes a cow or horse or ox would be picketed nearby. If there was any other life about, it would be a few chickens, for they were early added to the possessions of the new settler. They helped greatly toward supplying food for the family. We were very grateful for chickens in our first days in Kansas, when we had so little. For several months we bought all the eggs we wanted for five cents a dozen.

One thing I liked to do when we lived in the shanty and were breaking the first furrows on the home farm, was to climb to the roof at night and sit there and look at the stars and the sky and think and dream of all the things I was going to do out here in this great big, free, wild country, that would surprise the staid old friends we had left back East. The howling of the wolves on every side and the cooing of the prairie chickens in the evening—these were things that filled my mind with impressions so vivid that nothing has taken their place. Sometimes mother would call to me and ask why I stayed up there so long, and my answer was always the same, "It is so beautiful and there is nothing else to do and nowhere else to go." And that was the truth.

People were coming into the country in goodly numbers and homes were being built rapidly, so a law was passed that cattle would not be allowed to roam the country in freedom as they had done for so many years. There were no fences, and arrangements had to be made for taking care of the cattle that were not used for the dairy or the farm work. There was grass aplenty for many cattle, but someone had to be responsible for keeping them on the grass and out of the wheat or cornfields.

Here and there a man who had a boy big enough to ride a pony and watch cows and who was yet too small to do much other work, would let it be known that he would herd cattle for the summer. That meant that the cattle could be brought to him the first of May and that he would be responsible for their food and safety for six months. The charge was seventy-five cents a head. It was not much pay, but the grass cost nothing, and a little boy could take care of two hundred head and earn a hundred and fifty dollars in six months, so it worked out all right. Mother and the boys decided to let Elmer try herding and they bought him a little black Texas pony, called "Texas" ever after, and a herd of two hundred cattle was collected.

Things went very well the first summer, so he tried it again the second summer and even the third. But the third year it became almost too much for everyone concerned. Pasture land near home became a little curtailed by new families, and the growing crops tempted the cattle. Mother and the boys could not build a corral strong enough to hold the cattle at night; they kept getting out and into trouble.

About six miles from home there was a large tract

of prairie almost unsettled, with plenty of running water. Why not send the herd upcountry to that pasture? The ground was looked over carefully. A bend in the creek promised to serve as a comparatively strong corral without a great deal of hard work. A fence was built from bank to bank and a dugout made in the side of the creek bank; then the herd and the herder were moved.

Elmer had a pretty lonely time of it. Noble stayed with him sometimes, but he was very little. One of the older boys went up as often as possible, and someone kept Elmer supplied with food from home. Things went nicely until near the end of the season, when the cattle became restless with the shortening of the pasture and began to get out at night. There were fields of corn and wheat not far away, and the cattle found them. The result was always trouble and damages.

If a man had been on the job, he would probably have been wakened by the stamping of the cattle, and he could have kept them from getting into the fields, but a child sleeps soundly. Elmer took to sleeping on the ground near the corral fence, with his saddle for his pillow. Even so, he was afraid he might not wake up, and it was so near the close of the season that we did not want anything to go wrong. Mother decided it would be best for me to go up and stay with him. I had my own pony, and we planned to have some good times through the remaining days, which we hoped would end our herding of cattle.

At night we put the ponies on the grass, and Elmer made his bed at one end of the corral while I slept at the other. Every night we had to get up at least once for those cattle, but we succeeded pretty well until about three days before the end of the season.

That night we went to bed and to sleep as usual. We will never know what happened, but we were awakened by a fearful gale. The clouds were black as pitch, and when a bolt of lightning crossed the heavens we saw that the corral was empty. Our cattle—four hundred—were gone. At this place the banks of the creek were very high and we were sure that no cattle would go out over the bank.

Without taking one moment to think or say a word, Elmer was off in the direction from which he heard the cattle. For awhile I could hear him calling to his dog, and then I could hear nothing at all but the noise of the wind. When a flash of lightning came, I saw the broken fence—and my own situation.

It seemed a long time, but it really was not very long until I heard the cattle coming my way. I knew they had stampeded. I was afraid Elmer might not be able to get out of their way in the darkness and would be killed. It was such an awful moment that I forgot to think about myself. There were those crazy cattle tearing right at me, and in another second it seemed they were all about me and I was in a pandemonium. They were running so fast they could not stop for anything, so over the high creek

bank they went, one after the other, no telling how
many. Why I was not swept down with them I will
never know. But neither Elmer nor I was hurt in the
least. The cattle had broken through the fence so
near where we slept that it is a wonder they did not
trample on us. Our guardian angels must have been
very watchful that night, for we were in grave
danger.

We sat about in the rain until morning, and then
tried to gather in our cattle. It was a sad day's work.
Several had broken their necks going over the high
bank, and the loss had to be made up by us. This
adventure finished the herding business for us. I
hardly think it could have been made a success anyway, after that summer, for people were beginning
to build fences for pastures of their own, and this
reduced the land that could be used for commercial
grazing purposes.

I have said that Uncle Amos and his family
(which was increased by one addition every year)
came to live in the same house with us. This was a
great mistake, as such things are likely to be. Uncle
tried to get plastering and carpentering to do, and
that left Howard and Dave to do the work on the
farm. This might have been satisfactory if he had
not found fault with them on every occasion, or if
he had sometimes taken a turn himself at the work
that had to be done. Naturally the boys rebelled
and this was a great worry for mother. However, a
change was soon made. Uncle Amos was not having

as much influence as he thought he was going to have, and he soon said the farm was too small for two families. He thought mother could manage by herself, and that he should go somewhere else and get a big farm for his growing family. They agreed to disagree, and mother and the boys kept the farm while Amos took the team of horses as his share and went off out West to Gove County. He had many hard experiences and came back several years later with less than he had when he left our home.

Not long after he was gone, some lightning rod peddlers came along and flooded the country with their wares. Mother was a victim, and the old house has been protected from the wrath of heaven through all these years by the timely act of those oily-tongued men. From these men mother also bought a team of horses. We named them Fan and Arch, and although they were not high-grade animals, they served us well. In later years, we added Charley and Selim. Selim proved to be balky, and after a year or so Howard traded him for an organ, to my very great joy and satisfaction. Charley was on the farm until he died of old age.

The boys had done a job of breaking sod for a man who found, when they were finished, that he could not raise the money to pay them. He had a measly looking little pony which he said they could take for their work, if they wanted to. The pony was a year and a half old when they got him; he was small for his age even then and he never grew any bigger. He was so weak that the boys could

hardly get him home on his own legs, but they dosed
him and rubbed him and cleaned him and did everything else they could think of doing for a pony, and
finally he became a treasure and a playfellow for us
all. We named him Bob, and the boys taught him to
do all sorts of cunning tricks. Good care made him
fat, and he grew a beautiful long mane and tail.

All of us loved to ride Bob, but particularly Leah.
She would go to the pasture, take hold of his mane,
climb over his head and onto his back, and then ride
him all over the pasture. She almost met her Water-
loo that way. We never knew what had happened,
but we found her lying beside a haystack, unconscious. All she could remember was that she had
been on Bob's back in the pasture. Other horses were
there, too, and they started to run. This frightened
Bob and he started to run with them. Leah had not
broken any bones, but it was some time before she
wanted to ride again.

Leah had other experiences in connection with
Bob, but these were the result of her own independent spirit. She used to take the pony and ride away
without telling mother. One day she rode all the way
out to the herd—six miles. No one knew where she
was until she came straggling in late in the evening.
Mother told her over and over again that she must
not do this, but her words had little effect. Finally
mother said she would not talk about it any more;
instead, she gave Leah a good whipping and tried to
make her promise she would not do it again. They
had a terrible set-to. Leah would not promise, no

matter how much she was whipped. "You can kill me," she said, "but you can't make me say what I don't want to say!" Then she ran away, and mother picked up her milk pail and went to the barn, crying.

I have often thought about that since. Leah was just a little girl, but she was often left alone at home all day long. She amused herself as best she could in the house, but when she found she could get on the pony and go wherever she wanted to go, she naturally took advantage of the opportunity. She was really safe enough, but on the other hand, mother never felt quite easy about leaving her, and so when she came home and found no Leah, her conscience hurt and her fear mounted. But she never succeeded in making Leah understand that side of it.

When September came, I went to Abilene to go to school. Mother found a place for me to work for my board, with a family named Burns. They had one small child. I was expected to do all the work —washing, ironing, and cooking the morning and evening meals. The midday meal was taken downtown. I got up as early as two o'clock on washing and ironing days, so I would not be late for school, and even then I had to hurry. These people were as kind to me as they knew how to be, and there was enough to eat, but they both drank a good deal of beer and whiskey.

Breakfast had to be ready for the table by seven o'clock. They would bathe and dress and then call to tell me they were coming. That meant that I had to make each of them a whiskey toddy and they would be on hand to drink it while it was hot. (Later, when I was at home and someone was not feeling well, I said to mother that I did wish I had some good brandy or whiskey so I could make a toddy—that would help. Mother looked at me in amazement and asked what I knew about making a toddy. I told her it was one of many things I had learned during the few weeks I worked for my board.)

The house in which the Burns's lived was a long, narrow barn of a building, two stories high. The railroad track was not far from the front of the house and there was an alley on each side. It was one of the oldest houses in town and had been the most important one when it was new. Wild Bill Hickok made it his headquarters when the cattle center of Kansas was in Abilene. When I worked there, a few people still spoke of the house as Wild Bill's Hotel. In one of the rooms upstairs there were a lot of black spots on the floor; these were pointed out as the relics of a murder committed there the last night Wild Bill stayed in the house. There were no sidewalks near the place and sometimes we waded through mudholes to get home. The upper part of the house had once been painted red and the lower part gray, but that must have been years before. All in all, it was about as unlikely a place to live as can be imagined. The inside walls were plastered, however, so we were warm and comfortable. The Burns's lived upstairs in this house.

If one entered from the front of the house, one had to go through a long, dark hall to get to the kitchen; and although the back stairs were not far from the kitchen door, they led into the alley which was even less inviting than the dark hall. All the time I lived there I was afraid. I was afraid of Mr. Burns for he looked at me in such an ugly manner and said such queer things.

I had to hang the washing in the alley and, as I usually did this before daylight, I invariably had a chill before I was through, but this was more from fear than from cold. Before long I was not sleeping or eating properly and could not remember my lessons. When mother came to see me, I told her the whole story and she realized I was doing more than I was physically able to do. Mrs. Burns could not, I am sure, have been blind to this fact herself; but when mother spoke to her about it, she said I was not satisfactory and that she must get someone else.

Downstairs in the same building lived a family named Kreider. The husband was named Aquilla and the wife Priscilla. They had seven small children, and when mother told Mrs. Kreider that she had to hunt another place for me, she offered to take me in because, from what she had seen of my work, she felt sure I could be of value to her. I made the move, and although it was pretty hard for me, I kept the place until April. The unhappy thing about this family was that they thought only of themselves and felt that they were mistreated by everybody. I was not unkindly treated, however. I did not have to work so many hours, and there was time for me to study in the evening. I did get up first every morning to start the fire in the kitchen and in the sitting room and, while the family dressed, I prepared the breakfast. That was no hardship for me, but I got so homesick in this place that mother found a room for me and let me board myself until school was out that spring.

It was a wonder I didn't get sick, for my food was not what it should have been, my room was cold, and I had no exercise except walking to and from school. I had no money and was obliged to get along on the food mother brought me from home. She had very little to bring in the first place, and it was a long time between her visits. However, in spite of the drawbacks, I finished the year in good standing, though I had made no friends. I went from the bottom to the top in my class, and Mr. Jewett congratulated me, but I must have looked odd and out of place, for the others scarcely ever spoke to me. I had a brown delaine (wool) dress with large black dots on it, trimmed in black alpaca; it was made with a "Garibaldi waist." The belt, to which the skirt and waist were fastened, was black, and the neck was finished with a plain black band about an inch wide. I never wore a collar of any kind. I had no other dress to my name and wore this one every day through the winter. To save my dress, I had two big, highly colored plaid gingham aprons, made with a bib that buttoned back of the neck.

This is the way I attended the Abilene high school

for two winters. How did I ever do it? What a fine group of young people they must have been not to have driven me away by ridicule, or else what a freak I was not to be crushed by their indifference! It was terrible, but I did want to be able to teach school, and to do that I must go to school. I knew very well I could have no more than I had, so I shut myself up within myself, saw nothing and heard nothing, but just studied as hard as ever I could. When school was out in May, I went to work for Am Jeffcoat and stayed there until mother needed me at home to help with the wheat harvest.

When the wheat was harvested, there was no place to store it, so it was taken to market. On this occasion, mother again proved her unusual ability and stamina. She put most of that wheat into two-bushel sacks and loaded them on the wagon for market—more than most women and many men could have done. The next morning Howard and Dave hauled most of the wheat to Clay Center, twenty-one miles away. It was pretty hard work for two little boys, but they got from eighty cents to a dollar a bushel for it, and they were happy to bring home the money to their mother after a hard day on the road.

Uncle Rell had been out to see the folks in the wintertime and was delighted with everything. The next year grandfather and grandmother (Heikes) came and they were more than delighted with Kansas. Indeed, it was on account of the enthusiasm of her visitors that mother came by much of her trouble in after years. The wheat crop paid for the home at once, and grandfather thought he had never seen money made so fast. He was anxious to help mother get money to invest in more land, and this he did. A whole half section was added to the home quarter on the south and east, which subsequently was lost. But this is getting ahead of my story.

In the fall, I tried to get back in the Abilene schools again, but the Board had ruled that only residents could attend without paying a fee of two dollars and a half a month, and this mother thought we were not able to do. I worked at a hotel (Bun's) for my board for one month, but at the end of that time Mr. Jewett said I would have to pay or leave. (I am sure the same rule was in force the previous year, but seeing how anxious I was to get an education, Mr. Jewett did not report my case.) I went home. I would not go to the home school because I thought I knew more than the teacher did. This was a very foolish idea, but mother supported me in it and I again worked for Am Jeffcoat, whose wife had died and left him with four little children from one to eight years of age. His old mother came to live with us and she was more of a bother than a help. I think I would have been able to get on much better alone. Nevertheless, I stayed all winter, took care of the children and did the cooking, washing and mending. I also attended to the milk and sometimes did the milking. For this work I received two dollars a week and that was considered big wages.

Chapter 11

I FOUND a little time to study while I was with the Jeffcoats, but, more important, I met one of their friends who came to call. This was Mr. Probasco, a member of the school board in his district. School had not opened that winter because the children were too small, and now the board was looking around for a teacher for the spring term. I told Mr. Probasco that I intended to teach school just as soon as I could, whereupon he asked if I would take their little school for two months. He said they would pay me as much as I was getting for housework, and that he knew where I could work for my board. I went to see the other members of the school board and they said I could have the school and that my pay would be $4 a week. I took the position most gladly and began to teach on April 1, 1879. I was not quite sixteen. I worked for my board at Tom Perry's and so was able to keep all the money I earned. At the Perry home there were three children and two hired men. The house had one room and a shed kitchen with nothing overhead but the roof. It was very much crowded and there were some embarrassing situations, but the days went by, and I stayed until the last day and made a success of my school. When I went for my check it was made out for $36 instead of $32—just to show me they appreciated my work, they said. I was asked to take the school for the coming winter term, but I had a chance to get a longer term elsewhere, so I refused the offer.

I went to Abilene for one month of Institute work and in October I took the Zook School for six months at $25 a month. I boarded at Hershey's a mile and a half from the schoolhouse, and paid $2 a week board. I did a lot of knitting and crocheting that winter and knit enough scarfs and gloves and mittens to pay for my board, which gave me a great deal of satisfaction. In April I went back to my first school for two months at $25.

This school was six miles from home, and I rode Texas, the black pony, to and from school. One day Texas threw me and my foot caught in the stirrup. She ran and dragged me until my clothing was badly torn, but she did not kick me. She had become frightened at a pack of wolves that ran out from behind a hill. When I came to my senses, I thought about the wolves and wondered if they would come after me, but they had disappeared. I walked a mile to the nearest house where I went to bed for the day. Word was sent to school that I was hurt and would be absent. The pony went back to the folks as evidence of what had happened, and Elmer came for me late in the evening. The next morning I rode Texas to school as usual, and never fell off again.

After finishing my second summer term, I went

to Clay Center for a two months' Institute and met
the Clay County Superintendent of Schools. In
October I went back to the Zook school for six
months at $30 a month and stayed again with the
Hersheys. In March I had a letter from the Clay
County Superintendent asking me to apply for a
school in Clay County that was to have six months
of school during the summertime. I finished my
Zook school on the last of March, a Friday, and
began on the following Monday in Clay County.
The children were all small and we had a nice time
together. Here I learned that I could not say the
Lord's Prayer in school, for half of the people were
Catholic and asked that I omit it.

I finished this school on a Friday in September
and on the following Monday I was back in the
Zook school for another six months at $35 a month.
So it came about that I taught every school day of
that whole year, and I never thought of being tired
either.

All the time I taught at Glenwood—(so we had
named the Zook school, and it goes by that name
today)—I spent the weekends at home. One of the
boys would bring the pony and get me on Friday
evening and take me back on Sunday evening or
Monday morning. Just three weeks of the third term
had passed when, on getting home Friday night, I
found a letter. It was from the Clay County Superintendent, Mr. Starkweather. He said there was an
opening in the city schools and he wished I would
come up on Saturday morning and take the exami-

nation for it. Mother and I talked about it and she thought I ought to make the effort. I had a pony of my own named Daisy—a dear, ugly thing she was, but an easy rider and reliable and trustworthy.

It was twenty-one miles to Clay Center. It was the last of October and the weather was the Indian Summer kind that Kansas knows so well. I was up and off at three o'clock Saturday morning. My excitement was so great that I could not eat a bite of breakfast. Mother saw me off and wished me success. I was in Clay Center at seven o'clock and could not see the County Superintendent before eight. I should have gone somewhere and eaten some breakfast, but I had never eaten a meal at a public place in my life. I had been in the hotel in Abilene for a month, but all I knew about was the serving and the washing of dishes. I did not know how to go about getting food, so I wandered around until I could see Mr. Starkweather.

I called promptly at eight and he was ready and went with me to see the City School Superintendent, Mr. Copley. He came to the door and Mr. Starkweather introduced me to him. He said, "But, Madam, we have not had our breakfast! Come back at nine o'clock." And he shut the door in our faces.

Mr. Starkweather went back to his home, and I walked up and down the street in sight of Mr. Copley's home wishing for nine o'clock to come.

I had succeeded nicely with my teaching in the country and the simple folks were fond of me and thought I was all right, so it had not occurred to

me that I might be out of place in town. My best
dress, which was of cheap brown cotton trimmed in
red, did not look very well when I compared it with
the clothes of the girls who passed me on the street;
they looked so trim and fresh. For a little while, I
was about to give it all up and go home. I was having too much time to think. But the City Superintendent saved me from further deliberations by opening his door and beckoning for me to come in.

The breakfast dishes were still on the table. He
asked me a few questions, looked me over and smiled,
saying "You may get to work pretty soon." Then
he gave me a pencil and paper and told me to be
seated at the table. He pushed back the dishes to give
me room. The first list of questions was on arithmetic. That was not hard. History followed, and it
was harder for me. Then geography, which I did not
mind. After that I read to him. Without leaving his
seat, he threw a list of fifty test words before me. I
went over them very hurriedly and handed back the
paper, asking at the same time if I might be permitted to go right on with the work without stopping for dinner. He looked at me in surprise and said,
"You cannot have finished that list of words." "Yes,
sir, I have," I replied. I can see his look now as he
took the paper, gave a little grunt, and said, "We
want to have our dinner pretty soon. You go out for
an hour and then come back and finish the examination." I went out of the door but I did not know
where to go.

Nobody had asked me to take off my hat so I

had worn it all the morning. Nobody had offered me
a bite to eat or a drink of water, although the Superintendent's wife, the hired girl and the baby had
been in the room off and on all morning and they
had eaten candy and cookies and had drunk water,
too. But nobody noticed my presence. I was a curiosity and nothing more. I know it now. It did not
occur to me to think anything about it then.

I went out as I was bidden to do, and for the
want of some place to go and not knowing any better, I betook myself to the outhouse at the back of
the lot and stayed there until the hired girl came out.
I asked if she was through with dinner and if she
thought I could go back to work and she told me
to go in.

Mr. Copley seemed to be kinder to me and let me
get to work at once. I could feel some change in him,
although I did not understand it. He gave me only
five instead of ten questions on the other subjects
and let me answer orally. A little after two o'clock,
he said, "You have done a good day's work and I
will let you off now. Look for a reply by Wednesday."

I dragged to the alley where I had left my pony
and, after giving her the feed I had brought from
home, I started away from Clay Center and headed
for home and mother. It was five o'clock when I rode
up to the door, physically and mentally exhausted.

As I thought about the possibility of getting the
place, I grew more and more afraid I never could
teach in that beautiful brick building and get *forty-*

five dollars a month for my work! Of course I was
going to do something and be somebody *sometime*,
but as yet I had not been to school half long enough.
Surely I would have to know lots more than I did
to have so fine a place.

Wednesday came, and in the afternoon Howard
brought me a card. It read, "You passed all right.
Be on hand to begin work next Monday morning.
L. G. A. Copley." I was too excited for words.
After school I rode around the district calling on
three members of the school board. I told them of
my opportunity, showed them the card, and asked
them if they would release me and give the school to
Georgia Stewart. Georgia was about my own age
and had as much education as I did, and I thought
she was well able to handle the situation. At first
they would not listen to me at all, but on Friday
they met and agreed to let me go, giving Georgia the
place at $25 a month. I bade them all good-bye and
I never saw that school building again.

It was a marvel that the city place should have
come to me, and I will write here what I learned
later about it. Anyone who has a hobby is likely to
learn something valuable, and the time may come
when this knowledge will stand him in good stead.
This is what happened to me in connection with the
position in the Clay Center schools. At the opening
of the schools in September one more teacher was
needed. By that time of the year all the good teachers
had been engaged and it was not easy to find one.

An advertisement was put into the Clay Center

papers and private letters were sent out inviting teachers to come to the city and take the examination. Mr. Copley made out lists of questions for the applicants. There were a number of these on the first Saturday, but no one was given the position. More and more applicants appeared and took the examinations, and when I came along I was the fortieth. No one knew what the trouble was, but the problem became most lively and interesting to the people directly concerned. Of course I was ignorant of all this, for I had never seen a Clay Center paper, but when I tell you the story you will understand why people stared at me and why they spoke in my presence as if there was a question in their minds.

Mr. Copley had originally made out the list of questions without any serious intention of being unusually strict. This was going to be just an ordinary examination to get a new teacher to fill a place in the schools. But it happened that the words he chose for the spelling test were very difficult words, and some of the applicants could not spell even one of them correctly. Mr. Copley was a rather odd man at any time, and now and then he was something of a crank. As applicant after applicant failed on the spelling test, he became more and more irritated. Finally he said, "I will hold that place open until I find someone who can make a good score on that list of words and when I find her, she shall have the place."

After his patience had been well-nigh worn out, I appeared on the scene. The list of words was not

a fair list for the average person, but I don't believe
he was aware of that when he prepared the examination. I always thought that he simply pulled an
old speller from his shelves and jotted down a list
of fifty words, for it happened that I had studied
those very words from the Henderson Test Speller
and knew them perfectly. In fact, I had more than
once spelled every word in the book correctly. So you
see, my success was not especially to my credit, for I
could not have missed those words under any circumstances. They were a part of my very self, but
Professor Copley did not know that, and so the
"country greeny" won the place fairly on the basis
of his resolve.

Mother thought the best plan for me would be
to get rooms and do light housekeeping, taking Leah
with me. We three left home early Saturday, arriving in town soon after breakfast. It did not take
long to find a room that we thought would do, and
into it we put all the things we brought from home.
We went together and bought a tiny stove, which
answered for heating as well as cooking purposes
ever after. When mother left us late in the afternoon,
we were quite well settled and ready to begin work.

The next morning we dressed in our best and
went to Sunday School and church at the Baptist
church. This was Mr. Starkweather's church and
he had asked me to come. We became regular attendants and some time later Elmer and I were baptised
and joined the church.

I was so anxious to begin my teaching that Sun-

day seemed a very long day, and I found myself at
the schoolhouse so early on Monday morning that I
had to wait outside for the janitor to open the building. I was accustomed to being early enough to build
the fire and clean the blackboards before any of the
pupils arrived, so I had the habit of being on hand
early, for to me this meant getting things started
right.

For a few months at the beginning of my school
life I had been in the graded schools, but I remembered little about them, and all the time since then
I had lived and worked in the country. After I had
been introduced to twelve nicely dressed teachers as
"the new teacher" and watched 600 children come
up the steps and file into the various rooms, and
when finally all was still and the Superintendent
quietly said, "Now I will take you to your room,"
I had the biggest surprise of all.

I followed demurely, not knowing what would
happen, and found myself facing forty-five children
all in the First Reader. The number did not appall
me. I could have managed them if they had been
divided into different classes, but all of them were
in *one* class. The shock was almost too much for me.
How could I ever, ever keep them busy? The Superintendent took in the situation and went away.

Miss Allaway, a school girl of fifteen who had
been filling the place, was about to follow, but some
good angel spoke to her and saved me from a real
collapse. Her hand was on the doorknob when she
said kindly, "Would it be of any help to you if I

stayed this morning and showed you what we have been doing?'' To this day I have not ceased being grateful to her for those words and the good deed that followed. I spoke very quickly and earnestly and honestly. "I should be very glad if you would,'' I said, and she stayed.

I wasted not a moment; I watched her every movement and caught her every word. When noon came, I knew that I could do it, too. It did not take me long to get the idea. In a few days I was at work in earnest, so it was not very long before Mr. Copley said I was the most enthusiastic teacher in the building and that he had never seen anyone pick things up so rapidly as I did. When the spring came and a delegate was to be chosen to go to a teacher's meeting in Beloit, I was unanimously chosen to represent our Clay Center school. Mr. Copley wrote a note of introduction for me in which he said, among other things, "I predict a very successful future for this young teacher." Everyone was kind to me. All the teachers praised my work and the children loved me, and I was very happy.

My clothes did not look much like those worn by the other teachers, but it did not worry me. I did not have anything else, and anyway I had but one ambition and that was to succeed in my school. I was never invited to a party except at the church, and this was no more an invitation to me than to others, but I felt I could go, and did.

I had one distinction, however, before my first year was over, that was the envy of the other teachers. More children invited me home to dinner than all the other teachers put together.

Leah lived with me this first year and she was in my class at school. We lived in a house with a woman doctor who came home at all hours of the night; sometimes she was stupidly drunk for days on end. It was a most unpleasant situation and sometimes we were afraid, but nothing happened to us.

The second year I was promoted and given a very welcome five-dollar raise in salary. I was the only teacher who received an advance that year. The third year they raised my salary again, but Mr. Copley had left us and I was not happy with the man who came to take his place.

I was planning more and more definitely to go to school for awhile to get a better education. As a step in that direction, I decided to go to Holton, Kansas, during my third-year vacation to attend Campbell University for the summer term.

Chapter 12

IT WAS during those weeks at Holton, in the summer of 1883, that I met my husband, and I liked him *very* well at our first meeting. He was over six feet tall and, at that time, weighed about 140 pounds. The boys and girls called him my Longfellow. He was very kind to me and took an interest in my work.

Professor Menninger had come to Holton the year before from Indiana, to teach at the new Campbell University at Holton. It happened that he had to spend his summer vacation there, too, for he was helping with a survey of the town. We saw each other now and then at the institute socials. One feature of the institute was a reading contest, and I allowed myself to be persuaded to enter it. There was practicing to be done, and for this we went to the courthouse. It was a nice place for the young people to go, and when we finished practicing, it was quite natural that we should walk about awhile for exercise and pleasure.

I roomed in the same house with a young woman whose first name resembled mine. She was a prominent teacher in the county and a very good reader. When Professor Menninger walked home with us after our reading practice, we all three had a good time. He called at the house several times and once he took me for a beautiful ride. That ride created quite a stir and lost me the young woman's friendship.

It seems she was very fond of the tall professor and, more than that, she thought that he cared for her. I was not aware that I had gotten in her way, and it never occurred to her that he was interested in me. I was just tolerated on those walks because I happened to be with her. She had perhaps some basis for believing this for he had taken her to several places during the month—a favor not accorded me. But one day an invitation came from him asking *me* to go with him to a picnic. My friend was in a rage and said it must be a mistake, that she knew the invitation was intended for her. I was almost foolish enough to allow her to answer it, but I wanted to go so much that I talked to our landlady about the matter. She said she did not think it was a mistake at all, but even granting it was, if the professor was foolish enough to ask the wrong girl, he ought to go through with it, and if I wanted to go with him, I should accept the invitation.

I hesitated no longer, but wrote him that I would be glad to go. There were four of us in a two-seated carriage. I do not remember the name of the place where we went to eat our picnic lunch, but we had a delightful ride and a very good time. The day was far too short, but the memory of it has lasted through the years.

The professor and I agreed to write to each other, and at Thanksgiving time, "Prof," as I called him, came to Clay Center to visit me. We drove down to see mother and the old home. Mother liked "the tall gentleman" very much; this pleased me and I told her that someday I was going to marry him. She could not quite see why I wanted to do that. There was a nice young man from Abilene who came to see me frequently and he had asked mother if he could ask me to be his wife. Mother was very happy about this; she thought he would make an ideal husband and son—and then, too, he was a very promising young businessman, and that appealed to mother. I agreed that Sam was a fine young man and I liked him very much, but I did not think I could marry him. At any rate, there was no comparison between the degree of my interest in the two men in question.

Mother said she was sorry and that, of course, I could do as I pleased; but she thought that any girl who could earn as much money as I could and who was able to support herself and be independent, was foolish to marry any man. It seemed to her that a girl's chances for doing things were often handicapped by marriage. She warned me that "as you make your bed, so you must lie in it," and that I would have no one but myself to blame if I was unhappy.

Her words did not disturb me very much. I was sorry not to have her cordial and unqualified approval of my plans, but apparently she couldn't give it. At any rate, we enjoyed our visit to the country and got back to Clay Center Sunday evening. We invited my best friend, Susie Allaway, and her beau to call, and the four of us had a happy evening together. Prof should have left for Holton at four o'clock Monday morning, but he missed the train—at least, that was what he wired to the president at Holton. He spent all day Monday with me and we visited the town and the schools.

That winter was memorable for the letters we exchanged; we wrote very often. At Christmas he sent me a beautifully illustrated copy of Dante's *Inferno,* which I still have.

This was the second winter Elmer had been living with me. He attended the high school and not only paid his own tuition but earned a little extra by helping with the janitor work at the school. Before the year closed, I decided not to continue teaching another year in Clay Center. I felt that I should go to school somewhere for awhile, and Elmer could come with me. We had just about decided to go to Emporia, where a friend, Alfred Docking, was studying at the time. But when school closed in Holton at the end of July, Prof came to Industry to see me. He stayed a week and by the time he was ready to leave, Elmer and I had made up our minds to follow him to Holton.

We intended to board ourselves, for the sake of economy, and we took with us just as few things as possible. With the assistance of the Prof, we found two attic rooms in the home of Mr. and Mrs.

Weiss—interesting old German people. The rooms were small and the ceilings sloped; we could only walk about in the center without bending over.

The fall and winter were delightful. Elmer and I got along nicely with our work and loved it. Charley, it was Charley now instead of Prof, came to see us often and that pleased us. He brought his books with him and we all studied together, but he spent a great deal of time helping us instead of getting his own lessons.

In the first few weeks it never occurred to me that anything could be out of joint, we were so happy together. But before long I sensed antagonism that I could not understand. Now and then a word or a look or a slight showed me that the girls at the school were jealous of the attentions Charley showed me. And there were many attentions, for Charley was kind and thoughtful. Often we found fruit or candy on the table when we came home from school; we always knew how it came there, and we were grateful for these welcome additions to our meals.

The three of us lived in a dream of delight and if people had only minded their own business we could have gone on just as we were. But our association with Charley seemed to disturb some folks so much, and Charley would not agree to limit his calls to once during the week and on Sunday, so we decided that the best thing to do would be to marry, although I would continue going to school. We wrote our families about it and got their consent and, on the evening of January 15, 1885, we were married. This was on a Thursday, near the end of the winter term.

/ There were no prenuptial preparations. Charley bought a new tie and I had a fresh piece of lace for the neck of my green wool dress. I am sure that neither of us thought of a ring.

We were married at the home of the President, J. H. Miller, and only the faculty members attended the wedding. Mr. Ellis, the Baptist minister, was to marry us at seven o'clock, but he did not arrive. I think he forgot about it. / Finally Elmer was dispatched to find out why he did not come—there was no telephone in those days—and he soon returned with the minister. The weather was so cold that Elmer froze both his ears, and he used to say his ears tingled all winter in memory of our wedding. /

After the ceremony we put on our wraps and hurried to the chapel. It was the night of the term finals. After the program was finished, President Miller announced very humorously that we had been married that evening and had come out to receive the congratulations of our friends. He hoped they would all join in giving us a good time. They all came around to shake hands with us and we had a jolly time—students and faculty, Charley and me. The faculty gave us a yellow glass pitcher and two glasses as a wedding present.

We all left the building together, everyone teasing us, as you may imagine. Not far from the walk was an abandoned well, five or six feet deep. The hole was not plainly visible because the snow was so deep. Somehow we were pushed too close to it and Charley fell in. What fun the boys and girls had over that—then and for a long time afterward!

Charley came home with Elmer and me to our little attic rooms and the next day he brought over his trunk and books and we began our life together. On Tuesday morning we started the new term, going on with our work as before. Only now Charley and I went and came and stayed together—and we have done so ever since. We were very happy through those days and, for that matter, we have always been happy.

I do not remember that we were ever discouraged, although neither of us had anything but our ambitions. We had no furniture and no dishes. Before we were married we had bought an extra knife and fork and spoon for Charley, and we either dished food from the skillet or kettle onto our plates or else we set them on the table. We did not have a single extra anything. We lived on less than a dollar a week each all that winter, but we had enough to eat and we were comfortable. Charley was getting $40 a month for teaching, but he needed that to pay a back board bill which had accumulated the year before when he had received no pay at all. He had taken the advanced course and had taught a class or two to meet his tuition expenses.

Not long after we were married, my brother Howard and Cora were married. For their wedding trip, they came to Holton to see us. Howard's marriage changed the conditions at home and led to a

Professor Menninger and Bride, March, 1885   The Author on Graduation frcm Campbell University, 1886

new venture which started the first of April. I shall
have to go back a little to explain.

When mother bought the half section of land
south and west of the old home, cattle were bringing good prices. Her plan was to fence the land and
pasture cattle. The fence was built, the cattle were
bought and there were great hopes for the future.
But to accomplish all this, she had mortgaged the
land to the limit.

Then things began to go wrong. Cattle immediately depreciated in value and ours were finally
sold for less than they had cost and mother had
nothing for the grain that had been fed them. Grasshoppers, chinch bugs and drouth took the crops.
And all the time she had to pay interest on that
awful mortgage. No story setting forth the horrors
of a mortgage could ever seem too strong to me. I
know it is good for people to have something that
compels them to save money, but I don't ever want
anything to do with a mortgage again.

Everybody worked just as hard as he could—
mother hardest of all. She spent her days in the fields
at all sorts of labor and did the cooking and washing
and other housework at night. Every cent I could
spare went toward the interest on the mortgage.
Howard and Dave, like all other boys, wanted
money and there was none to give them. Their
choice of associates was not fortunate and some of
their friends finally became the cause of their leaving
home. After awhile they came back, but now they
were men and insisted on doing things the way they

wanted to do them. They had seen *men* doing things and they were eager to have their try. Mother was so afraid that they would leave her again that she was ready to accept them on almost any terms. But their judgment was immature and conditions generally were so bad that financial matters became hopelessly involved. Mother had to give up the fight and let the cherished half section pasture go for the mortgage. She was almost crazy over her own losses and, to make matters worse, she had also lost the money her father had invested in the land. This was early in 1885, the year in which Howard and I both married.

As I have explained in the Foreword, I wrote up to this point in my story in August, 1899. In March, 1921, I began again and carried the story on from 1885 to 1921.

Chapter 13

AFTER Howard was married, on March 10, 1885, it seemed best that he run the farm on shares and live in the old home. Mother decided to come to Holton and keep boarders. We would live with her, which would help out all around. We found an eight-room house that seemed suitable; the roomers were to use the upper part and the basement could be the dining room. The price was $2000, ten per cent down. We borrowed the money at the bank in our own name and, I think, on our cheek, for we had nothing to give as security. We just undertook to do what we could and hoped everything would be all right. When the purchase was arranged, mother drove down overland and settled in the house in April, 1885.

Elmer and I continued with our schooling. Our college course was divided into three years of eleven months each. Our only vacation was the month of August, for school began on September 1 and ended on July 31. There were five terms in the eleven months, four of ten weeks each, and one, through June and July, of eight weeks. The first year's studies were called the teacher's course, the second year's, the scientific course, and the third year's, the classical

219

course. Elmer and I finished the teacher's course July 31, 1885.

My husband's folks, who all lived in Tell City, Indiana, were so anxious to see what kind of wife Charley had selected that they asked us to pay them a visit during our vacation. Charley wrote that we would have to wait another year because we had no money. His father replied by sending us $50. For the first two weeks of our vacation, we went to Verdon, Nebraska, where Charley taught in an Institute two weeks, for which he received $50. Then we went on to Tell City for the last two weeks of August, seeing and being seen by all the folks.

They were very kind to us, and the visit was delightful. I must have seemed very "western" to them. I wanted to go everywhere my husband went and do everything he did, and they did not wholly approve of this. I went fishing, and hunting for blackberries, and I tried to row a boat with my husband. They thought those things were only for men. But I loved to be on the move every minute, and we both had a good time.

We were always being offered wine and beer on this visit, and it shocked me. Charley had tried to tell me what I would find in his home and among his people, but still it was rather a surprise. We refused the offers of such refreshment and in a day or so friends stopped asking us to join them. But every day brought some occasion for a slap at Kansas and her "prohibition that did not prohibit." On the Sabbath we were all at home, having a fine time together. After awhile, father came in with glasses and several bottles of wine. He said he was bringing us his very best, and he told us how old the wine was. He wanted everybody to drink with him. Charley said we could not do it.

Then there was a most unhappy scene. Father felt he had been greatly insulted by his own son— his mother criticized him for spoiling the happy occasion, and his brother and sisters could not understand why he should choose to rebuke them all in so rude and unkind a manner. Father said he would never ask us to drink with him again, and Charley said he hoped we might all live to see the day when Indiana would think that Kansas was on the right side of the question. His family could not believe it would ever be so, but it was. Not many years later, father took great pleasure and pride in talking about his prohibition son in Kansas. He admitted he believed that prohibition was right and just, and he hoped it might spread throughout the country.

In September, Charley went back to the college to teach, and Elmer and I embarked on our second year, that is, on our scientific course. The college was short on its teaching staff, so President Miller gave me the privilege of earning my tuition by teaching two subjects each term. I taught Geography, Algebra and Mechanical Drawing. This was quite a help financially, and I liked the work.

We had planned that when Elmer finished his college course, he and Charley would go into the law together, so they bought some standard law texts

and spent all their spare time reading them. Charley
had met a young lawyer named Scott Hopkins and
had already spent some time in his office reading
law. Naturally, Elmer wanted to do the same thing.
We were all intensely interested and were happily
anticipating the days to come.

Our schoolwork was getting on splendidly, but at
home things were bad. Mother was brokenhearted
over her losses; she was completely discouraged and
spiritless. She did not know a thing about running
a boardinghouse except what she had learned by
boarding farm hands. She thought the students
were hard to please and that irritated her. She
charged only $2 a week for board, and no matter
how little things cost, it was impossible to realize
any profit on this small sum. Mother could think
only of her boys, her home, her debts and her troubles, and that was hard on us all. During the spring
of 1886, her father and mother came to see Kansas
a second time, and although it was fine to have them
with us and they enjoyed everything, it was hard on
mother because one of their objects in coming to
Kansas was to see if mother couldn't arrange somehow to pay back the money grandfather had invested with her.

Their visit really finished mother with the boardinghouse business. She felt she *must* get back to the
farm, so she left Holton in June, and turned the
house over to Charley and me. When she had bought
the house, there was furniture in the rooms we intended to rent, so mother had brought with her from

the farm only the little she needed. When she gave up the house, she put her goods into the wagon and drove home with Leah and Noble. It was a rather difficult task to undertake the management of a dormitory even though it was not very large, and to teach three classes a day and study besides, but I did it, and Elmer and I both finished the scientific course on August 1, in good shape—he with higher grades than I.

In fancy work, darned net had become the rage, and I took the fever. I had begun early in the year 1885 to make myself a dress for my graduation the following year. That summer I had carried the dress with me to Verdon and worked on it every minute while my husband taught in the Institute; and I carried it to Tell City, where it interested the folks, but I didn't get very much done. Then on through the winter and spring I spent every spare moment darning this dress, finishing it in time for Commencement Day, August 1, 1886. Everyone thought it was wonderful, and all the girls were envious. I remember *that* about my Commencement, though I cannot recall who the speaker was nor anything he said. The dress is in my "keepsake box" today.

After Commencement, Elmer went home and worked on the farm. Charley and I still had the house on our hands, and something had to be done with it. Jackson County held its Institute in August, so I stayed at home and kept roomers who were in town to attend the Institute, and I also worked at getting the house in shape for the opening of school in September. During this time Charley went back to Verdon, Nebraska, and taught in the Institute again, this time for the entire month.

Elmer's stay on the farm did not last long. He was restless and uneasy and felt he ought to be earning something, but he intended to go to college September 1 for the final year, to complete the classical course. I had decided to accept an offer from Mr. Roop to teach in the primary department of the public schools. Flora Menninger, Charley's sister and Emma's twin, was coming to spend the year with us and attend the college. Charley was going to continue to teach. Among us we would keep house and take care of the roomers and save all we could toward a college law course for the boys in the coming years.

It was at just this time that the Rock Island Railroad line from Topeka to St. Joseph was being run through Holton. A man who could compute figures for the surveying gang was urgently needed. Elmer, back from the farm, was recommended to the management, and he was offered six dollars a day. It was a fine chance to earn large wages during vacation, and the money would help throughout the coming year. Elmer took the place, and we all considered ourselves very fortunate. If we had only known!

The men on this job boarded at a farmhouse which had a well lower than the barn sewage drain. They drank the well water. In a few weeks Elmer came home one Saturday evening sick with typhoid fever. So instead of working out our well-laid plans, we dragged through the weeks until he died. His illness was a great strain on us all. Most of the time he was delirious and someone had to be with him constantly. Mother came to us in November to help. Just before Elmer died, he sang "Let the lower lights be burning, send a gleam across the wave." He sang the entire verse in fairly good voice, and then he repeated the Lord's Prayer. Then he spoke his last words, "Now let us go to sleep." This was on December 19, 1886.

All the family came down for the funeral, and on December 21, with the loving sympathy of faculty and students, we laid Elmer's body to rest in the Holton Cemetery.

Elmer's death was a severe blow to us. It changed our plans, of course, but it was also very hard on our spirits. It was a long time before I could reconcile myself to the fact that he had to be taken—so young and so promising. Today, scientific methods do much to prevent typhoid cases but in those days it was a most dreaded disease and young people by the score died from it. Elmer was only one of several young men boarding at the farmhouse who died of typhoid that same season.

Christmas brought us little cheer. We thought it would be well to go to Topeka during the holidays to attend the State Teachers' Association Meeting. A number of our friends were going, so we joined them. We had to change cars at Valley Falls, and Charley agreed to buy the tickets for all the Holton crowd, while we went directly to the waiting train. But there were other people who wanted to get tickets also, and Charley politely waited until they had theirs. By then it was so near traintime that the agent was unable to get the tickets ready, so the train went on without Charley and without the tickets—eighteen or twenty.

For a time, we did not realize what had happened. When we reached the next station there was a message authorizing the conductor to pass so many from Holton, the tickets to follow by the next train. That meant that I had to go on without Charley— and I did not have one cent with me. I was ready to cry, when Mr. Roop, Superintendent of the Holton Public Schools, who was a great jollier, held up a twenty-dollar gold piece and said, "I'll give you this if you don't cry." Everybody laughed and it did not seem so bad.

One of the girls said she was going to stay with a friend and that she knew her well enough to take me along, so I was not left alone or comfortless. The Smiths took me in and when Charley arrived the next day, I preferred to stay with them rather than go to a crowded hotel with him. The Smiths came to be very good friends of mine when we moved to Topeka later on.

After the new year, it seemed very hard to accommodate ourselves to the new conditions. We each did our work and somehow managed to get our meals and do the things that had to be done every day. On

Saturdays I cleaned the rooms and did the washing and ironing for eight beds.

In order to realize as much as possible from renting rooms, we lived in the basement. It was not wholly underground, but it was not a cheerful place. Charley was not very rugged and after a time he acquired a cough so bad that it exhausted him on more occasions than one. The college was understaffed and there was almost no heat. In his enthusiasm, Charley thought he could do anything, and whenever a class was organized for some subject that was not on the list for assigned teachers, he accepted the job. During those years in Holton he taught Music, Telegraphy, Penmanship, Bookkeeping, Physiology, Natural Philosophy, Chemistry, German, Photography, Algebra, Geography, History, Geology and Botany! He did surprisingly well at everything, but he was working altogether too hard and under bad conditions. As the days went by, the strain began to tell on his health.

A few times we had the doctor call to see him and once he said, "What do you people intend to do next year?" I told him I thought we would teach school. Just at that time two school buildings had been finished at the Topeka State Industrial School and Charley and I had been offered the chance of taking charge of one of these buildings at $50 a month each. We were considering this proposition.

I told good old Dr. Adamson about it. He said, "Better not. You won't keep that husband of yours many years if he keeps on working as he has been.

Better get out of schoolwork." His warning was an
added worry to us but out of it grew the final decision as to my husband's life work. He resolved to
study medicine.

We felt that if we were to continue in school work
we could do no better than to stay in Holton, Charley teaching in the college and I in the public schools.
What we wanted was to work together in the same
school. Our most intimate friends in the college were
Mr. and Mrs. J. C. Brown. They were teaching together as they had been for many years, and we liked
them so much that they became our ideals. We devoted ourselves very closely to the business in hand.
Everything concerning the college or public schools,
and anything that they were trying to forward, we
supported enthusiastically.

I went to my first show during the winter of
1886. It was a performance of *Uncle Tom's Cabin*
given by a traveling troupe, and I think the tickets
cost thirty cents. It was given in the skating rink,
which was just an unplastered shed of a place, but I
enjoyed that play as much as anything I have ever
seen since. Later in the same year I saw "A Musical
Family"—consisting of father, mother and ten children. One number was a "laughing number." First
one member of the company laughed, then two, then
three, and then they all laughed together—and naturally the audience laughed with them. I thought
it was the funniest thing I had ever seen.

Charley wanted to join the Odd Fellows, but I
had been taught that secret societies were very

wicked, and I felt that to join one was almost like selling oneself to the evil powers. All the Menninger family belonged to the Odd Fellows, however, and finally I agreed to let Charley join. But I worried so much about it each time he attended a meeting that to please me and "keep peace in the family," he gave it up.

Except for these things, we had no entertainment at all. We had no time and no money, and although we had a house, it was not a home. And we wanted a real home, somehow, somewhere, as soon as we could get it.

Chapter 14

THE winter wore along and before July 31, when school closed, we had decided on our plans for the coming year. A new school building had been built in the west part of the town and I was reappointed to teach and assigned to the new Colorado building. Flora was going home, and Charley was to go to Hahnemann Medical College in Chicago. I was to furnish the means to keep him there. My salary was $45.00 a month, and there would be a little income from room rent, but that had to be saved to be applied on the house. We thought we could manage it. The check Charley had received for teaching at the Nebraska Institute paid the initial expenses.

It was with a world of hope we said good-bye to each other in September, 1887. Charley was going to study hard in Chicago and make a good doctor, and I was going to stay in the old house at Holton and teach my very best and send him all the money that I could to help him get ready to earn a home for both of us.

It was not so hard a winter as we thought it would be. We wrote each other twice each week. Neither of us could spare the time nor the postage to write oftener. I used to live from letter day to letter day, and I was interested in all the things he was doing in his schoolwork. The good grades and the preferences that he earned, and finally a prize or two, were all matters of special pride to me. Sometimes he would go to a good show, taking a seat in the gallery, and would write me all about it. I would be so thrilled and would think of the future when, he said, we would be going together. He saw *Faust*, with Henry Irving as Mephisto and Ellen Terry as Marguerite, at the McVickers Theatre. He also saw Edwin Booth in *Hamlet*. It was such interesting news to me.

About Christmastime two exciting things happened to me. First, I had an opportunity to sell the boarding house. It was like being released from prison. The man wanted possession immediately, and I was only too glad to let him have it. He took the house and everything in it but me. I rented two little upstairs rooms, near my school building, from Bob Moore—a man who made a name for himself in veterinary medicine and later became president of a veterinary college in Kansas City. The other big thing was my Christmas present from Charley—a sealskin cap. When I found it cost ten dollars, I did not see how he could possibly have saved as much as that. I used the cap for many years, and my sister Leah wears it now to do her chores on cold days.

I did not like to stay alone in the two little rooms, and I wanted Leah to go to school, so she came and lived with me until school was out in June.

Brother Dave was out of work and out of money, too, and seemed unable to find anything to do. I heard of a place where a man was needed, so Dave came to Holton and took the job of driving a dray wagon. He did not live with us, but we felt we could have his help if we needed it.

All the days were busy, happy ones. Leah did splendidly in her studies. My own work was a success. The Chicago letters were always an inspiration, and it was fine to be able to send the money to keep my husband in college. The winter slipped by rapidly, and from Christmas—when we left the old house—to February seemed only a few days, and yet when I remembered that Charley had been gone since September, it seemed a very long time. He was due home about midnight the last of February and Leah and I were anxiously waiting to see him. When he did come he was bubbling over with enthusiasm. It was hardly possible to think of going to bed, there was so much to say, to think about, to plan for.

Holton schoolteachers were given a day each term to visit other schools, but I had not used my days up to this time. Charley suggested that I go to Topeka for my visit and said that he would go with me and call on the doctors with a view to finding something to do. We went down on Thursday night. I spent Friday in Harrison School, and he visited several physicians. When we met at night he seemed to be acquainted with all of them and, furthermore, he had accomplished the thing he hoped for. Doctor Roby gave him permission to stay in his office during his vacation, and Charley thought this would be a great help to him.

We went back to Holton in the evening and spent Saturday and Sunday together. On Monday morning, Charley went to Topeka and found a room for himself at Tenth and Monroe Streets. He planned to take his meals at a restaurant.

Charley had not been there long before he decided that when he finished his college course he would locate in Topeka, and we agreed that in that case it would be a good idea for me to get a position in the Topeka public schools for the following winter, so that when he came home from college I would be settled there. I put in my application at once and took the examinations. In a few days, notice came that I had been assigned to the primary grade in Branner school. This was on Branner Street, near the Santa Fe tracks.

When my school was out in Holton, I joined my husband in Topeka and for a few weeks we had a wonderful time together. Of course, we could not be together every minute, and I did hate to sit or walk about alone in this strange place surrounded by strange people. But we had our meals together at the restaurants and had lovely walks in the evenings, and these things made up for the rest.

I spent the month of July on the farm, and in August my husband and I went back to the little rooms in Holton. Sue Hoaglin was Superintendent of the Jackson County Schools and she had an eye for new ideas and higher standards. She experimented in one direction by having me teach Primary Methods in the Institute. It was the first effort of this kind in the state, and was most successful. Mr. Roop was conductor and Charley was an instructor in the regular work. Mr. Roop was enthusiastic over my work and, as long as I would go, he took me somewhere every summer to repeat it. ✓

Today, of course, primary instruction is one of the Institute courses, but it was a novelty then.

Laura Ehrenfeld, one of my first Holton friends, stayed with us during this month. We crowded a world of activity into that month of August, 1888. Charley and I both realized that we would never live in Holton again, though it was full of beautiful memories and we loved it. We took all the walks our time allowed, visiting the interesting places and recalling the nice times we had had there together. When we went by a certain house where he and another professor first roomed in Holton, he told me how they had both suffered from the cold. Whether the house was a cold one or the owner was trying to save coal, they never knew, but they were always cold. They would hurry through their dressing to get to the dormitory dining hall for breakfast and hope for a little heat, but the dining hall was a big one, and if the morning was a very cold one it was cold too. So they would eat a scanty breakfast of a little mush, fruit and coffee, and hurry on to the school buildings, but even there they were not likely to find a comfortable recitation room. The heating system was not a success and none of the rooms was

ever too warm; some were never heated at all. Often
he worked day after day in the cold. Yes, the bitter-
est memory of his first year in Holton was the cold.

The woods back of the university was a delightful place to walk and it furnished the background
for much campusology. Through it ran a stream of
water with tiny waterfalls, mossy corners and fallen
logs. We loved this place and paid it more than one
visit in that last month. I am glad we did, for cruel
"civilization" has removed most of the trees and sub-
stituted houses.

Charley was a wonderful person to see everything. We never took a walk but he found some new
thing to show me, or he told me things he had
learned, or he found something worth taking home
to our little rooms. No matter how wilted our finds
might be, when we got home he was never too tired
to straighten them out, arrange them in the very best
way and put them into a vase as "a bouquet for my
best girl." We never had a better month in our
lives than that one, when we were working together
and dreaming of beautiful things for the future. We
thought of our first attic rooms as of faint dreams in
the long ago. We easily forgot the worry of the big
old boardinghouse. We thought of Holton as the
place that had given us each other, and we loved it.
Most of all, we loved the little rooms that we called
ours at that time. However, when the Institute work
was over, we were not sorry to pack the few things
we had accumulated, because it was a step toward

the realization of the home that was someday to be ours.

My trunk held all my needs. A few other things were shipped to Topeka and put into a storeroom. We got to Topeka a few days before the opening of school in September. Together we walked around and found a boarding place for me near the school in which I was to teach. Charley had left his trunk at the depot, and when he saw that I was settled for the winter, he left for his second year in Chicago.

I liked my new work and the novelty of my surroundings, and with two fat letters from Charley each week and two to write in return, I felt myself quite content. None of the other teachers in the building lived near the school. They did not think it was "the thing" to live with "those people." After school opened and I learned that I had made this great mistake, I was a little puzzled to know what would happen to me. If I had realized before that I would be counted odd for doing so rash a thing I suppose I would not have done it. As it was, I merely wanted to be near my school.

I found that the children had done very little reading. Very few in the first grade knew the simple Mother Goose stories. Fifth and sixth grade children had not heard of Louisa M. Alcott. I asked permission to use one room after school hours, and soon I was spending four afternoons a week reading to all who would stay. Many times the room could not hold them all. I began with *Under the Lilacs* and, during the year, read most of Miss Alcott's books,

and other stories. The interest was intense and the
results remarkable. Every now and then, someone
still introduces himself to me and reminds me of the
reading I did after school hours in Branner. It was
a worth-while thing to do and I am so glad it came
into my mind to do it.

I called at the home of every child in my room.
Many of the families were truly very poor and a
good many of them very shiftless, too. I used my
tithe to buy stockings and mittens and spent my Saturdays in the homes, mending stockings for some
tired mother or sewing or cooking. Sometimes I
would stay with the children so the mother could go
uptown. I went to a missionary meeting at the First
Presbyterian Church and asked them if they would
not gather up some old clothes for me to make over
for poor children. They sent me a great many and
continued to do so, and I could often help some
mother make or remake a very nice suit or dress for
her child. I was never so busy in my life. I kept up
my extra work at Branner for the three years I
taught there, but I was not quite so active after the
first year, for by that time somebody was looking
for me to come home when night came.

There were eight teachers in the Branner school.
Miss Chamberlain, the youngest, asked me one night
to go home with her and attend the Adams Chautauqua Circle. It was held at the First Presbyterian
Church and four of our teachers were in attendance.
Miss Chamberlain seemed to have a very active part
on the program, which was interesting from begin-

ning to end, but none of the girls introduced me to
a single person. I waited for Miss Chamberlain, who
was busy all evening until the door closed. One by
one the people passed me and went out. It was
almost the last person who stopped and asked if I
were a stranger. This was Mrs. Ed Whitaker, who
later became one of my good friends.

Charley came home in February, 1890, bringing
with him his certificate to practice medicine. He had
made arrangements to work for Dr. Roby for forty
dollars a month. We were to have two small, un-
furnished rooms and live in the office building. The
back room had two windows, one of which faced
the sidewall of the next building; the back window
opened on the tin roof of the lower extension of the
building, and on the alley. The bedroom was very
small. We bought a one-burner oilstove for such
cooking as we needed. When we were using it, it
stood on one of the "kitchen" windows. When it
was not in use, we pushed it behind the bed, which
space served as a storeroom.

Our table was two orange crates, one on top of
the other, to form a cupboard for all our kitchen
accessories. It was dressed up with a fancy curtain
and the top was covered with a bit of white oil-
cloth. A cup of coffee and a roll, or some kind of
light, prepared food, served for our morning meal.
We each had our lunch near our work, and we had
dinner together at some public eating place in the
evening.

At the close of the school term, we moved into

front rooms which we were able to make comfortable as well as pretty. Father had sent us a wedding gift of a walnut dresser. We brought this out of storage and added a folding bed, which had a long mirror and a writing desk for its front. With two chairs, a few little homemade rugs for the floor and white scrim curtains at the window, we felt very rich. The front room faced the street. The whole south end was one big bay window. We bought a ten by twelve rug and Father sent us a walnut bookcase. A few pictures and personal extras completed the room. (When we moved into 1251 Topeka Avenue in 1899, we sold the folding bed, for which we had paid $65, for $25. The walnut dresser was sold with the home. The big bookcase is still in the family.)

While I was teaching in Branner, Mr. Bloss was Superintendent of Schools. He was very much interested in my work and, at the meetings which were held every two weeks, had me give lessons to all the teachers of my grade. Some of the older teachers did not like this, but they seemed to accept it. Soon they were all my friends and I led my department as long as I was in the schools. Another honor occurred in the form of teaching a course in Mechanical Drawing once a month on Saturday morning. This class was open to all who were interested, and it was the most fun of all. We had a fine time and I liked it immensely.

Mr. John MacDonald was editor of the *Kansas State School Journal*. I have always thought it was

on account of Mr. Bloss that Mr. MacDonald came
to visit me in my school, where he seemed very much
pleased with everything he saw me do. He asked me
to write for his *Journal*. I said I did not know how
to write, but he replied, "Just write me a letter and
tell me how you teach Reading." He came frequently
to persuade me to write an article for the *Journal*. I
began during my second year in Branner and from
then until I quit teaching, I wrote a monthly note
for the *Journal* on Reading, Writing, Numbers, Object Lesson, Busy Work, etc. About the year 1890
a system of teaching Arithmetic, known as the
Grube Method, swept the country. Mr. MacDonald
used to say, "We put that over in the *Journal* several years ago," and we had, through my lessons
with the primary teachers, taught that method all
through the Topeka schools, not knowing what a
remarkable thing we were doing.

Charley spent every moment he could with his
books or with Doctor Roby, trying to learn things
he needed to help him in his profession. For me the
days were full with my schoolwork. To help keep
myself at real study, I took drawing lessons two evenings a week from a Professor Hopkins, who had
quite a large class in the building at 4th and Jackson. It was here that I met Fred Barton and his
mother. Fred was a young Santa Fe man, very much
attached to his widowed mother and to the church.
He helped me to find some very interesting friends at
a time when I was lonely and needed encouragement.

On one or two evenings each week during the time

we lived at the Roby's, I went to some sort of a
show, either at the Grand or at the Crawford Thea-
ter. I saw some very fine things, and how I did enjoy them! Mrs. Smith, the lady to whose house I
was taken when we came to the Teachers' Association meeting in 1886, was the wife of a newspaper-
man. She had passes for every show that came to
town and, evening after evening, she would telephone me and say, "If you want to see so-and-so,
meet me at the Grand or Crawford's at 8:15." Most
of the time I was on hand. The theaters were close
to our rooms, and I was not at all afraid, so Charley
urged me to go. I owe most of my little knowledge
of plays and players to the generosity of Mr. and
Mrs. Joe Smith.

Chapter 15

WE had moved to the Roby home in February, 1889, and we stayed there eighteen months. In very many ways, it was a wonderful period in our lives—we were so happy just to be together. But, after a year had passed, the natural urge to independence asserted itself and the situation we were in did not promise much of a future. Six months later we decided that we would set up an office of our own.

It was a risk, and so it was with a great deal of anxiety that we decided to take the two front rooms and one back room at 727 Kansas Avenue, at $35 a month. We took them, trusting Providence that it would come out all right, and moved the last of August, 1890. The very first day we were in the new rooms someone came in "to see the Doctor"— and in all the days from then to now, there have been few when no calls have come for "the Doctor."

We had a great deal of pleasure setting up housekeeping by ourselves. We had all the furniture we needed for the moment, and by the time cold weather came, we had enough money for a new base-burner. At the Roby's it had been hard to cook. Although the new home was not a great improvement, there were some advantages. I did not have to be quite so careful of the cooking odors. There was more room to work in, and when the base-burner was started, we did all sorts of cooking in the magazine and had the nicest kind of lunches after our day's work.

I kept on with my work at the Branner School, and sometimes we invited Miss Chamberlain, who also taught there, Miss Rohl and Miss Milligan to have a meal with us. Miss Rohl and Miss Milligan were Holton friends who had been invited to come to Topeka to teach, on my recommendation, and the three girls roomed together. They helped us to have many jolly times.

Mrs. Barton and Fred also came to call and asked us to go to the Presbyterian Church. We liked Dr. Ray, the minister, so much that we kept on going. Elmer and I had originally brought our letters from Clay Center and had joined the Baptist Church in Holton. After we were married, Charley went with us to worship there, although he had attended the Presbyterian Church before. I had had a class of little folks in the Sunday school, Charley had conducted the men's class and Elmer had a big class of young men, many of them much older than he.

Charley was really a Lutheran, but I did not wish to join that church. And he did not believe in close communion nor immersion, so we decided now to compromise and join the Presbyterian Church. This we did in 1891. We rented a pew quite far back in the church. It was all we could afford, although I do not remember the amount of the rental.

Not long after we joined the church, Mrs. A. L. Redden gave a big reception. She had not been living in her beautiful new home on Topeka Avenue very long, and this affair was to be an opening to show the place to her friends. She decided to invite all the women of the church and that included me. When my invitation came I never thought of accepting it because I had no clothes for that sort of thing, and I knew but one person who was to be there—Mrs. Barton. But Mrs. Barton said I must go with her, that my clothes were all right, so I went. It was the most wonderful thing I had ever seen. Such a spacious home and such wonderful gowns! Everything about it was amazing. There were so many women doing nothing but bowing and talking—no program of any kind—that I could not quite get the drift of it, but that did not bother me. There were introductions and polite phrases, and we were taken into the dining room which was full of music that sounded like an orchestra, but nobody was playing. I discovered that the sound came from a music box which kept on playing continuously.

We sat around the room and a handsomely dressed woman brought us ice cream, cake, nuts, coffee and candy. I thought it must be wonderful to have enough money to buy ice cream and cake for all that crowd. Then we went out to say good-bye to our hostess. She turned to an alcove filled with hundreds of pink, red and white roses, and asked me to take the one I liked best. It was most exciting and I did not want to leave so soon, but Mrs. Barton said we'd better go so the house would not be over-crowded. We had been there quite a while and, as over five hundred had been invited, many guests were still expected.

I walked back to our rooms in a daze. It had been so wonderful—*my first reception.*

Besides getting ourselves started, we undertook to send my brother Dave to a veterinary school in Chicago. He was not happy at farming and had left home, so he agreed to go to school, if we would help him. This meant about $50 a month for two terms of six months each, over a period of two years, but we managed it. In November we found that we had a few dollars' surplus and decided to begin saving something each week. We bought a little earthen barrel and into it we put every cent we did not have to use.

Business kept picking up all the while and by Christmastime, Doctor found he could not keep up with all his calls by walking and using the streetcar, as he had been doing. He talked to a friend, W. I. Miller, about it, and he said he had a horse and buggy which could be bought for $180. Mr. Miller said the amount of the down payment did not matter and that we could pay off the balance as we were able. It was at this point that we broke open the little jug and were surprised to find that we had $80 in it. It helped us realize that we *could* save a little, and that we could buy the horse and buggy. We felt very proud of that investment, and it was not very long before Mr. Miller received all his money.

I kept at my schoolwork and Doctor went out to make his calls, so we soon realized that there ought to be someone in the office while he was away. We advertised for a girl, and Sadie Dunn applied and was employed. We paid her $2 a week; her hours were eight to four, and she brought her own lunch. This was a very decided help. Sadie was with us for sixteen years and we were always fond of her.

When vacation time came, Charley stayed alone while I taught in the Institutes at Troy and Fort Scott. In September, 1891, I was transferred to Garfield School at my request, because it was so much nearer home. When spring came, we had saved $300. We thought we would like to have a home, and when we found we could make the first payment on a little cottage at 1270 Topeka Avenue with the money we had, we took the great step. A home of our very own! It was tiny indeed, but we loved it and it was a joy to put down carpets and hang up curtains. If I ever expressed the fear that we were undertaking too much, Charley would reply, "We can do it. I can pay for it."

It began to look as if I should soon quit teaching school if we were to have the family for which we had been planning for such a long time. I took my place in Garfield School in September, 1892, and taught until the holidays, when it seemed best for me to resign. I did my last teaching in December, 1892, having begun in April, 1879, so my school teaching career covered almost fourteen years.

In January, 1893, we began our homemaking in earnest. The little cottage had but one bedroom; there was no bath, no back porch, no barn. The barn we needed badly and the other things we wanted very much. My husband's practice kept getting better and better all the time, so we decided to make some improvements on the house. We built a kitchen and porch and bath and a little room just big enough to hold a bed. We built a barn, too. When it was all finished we thought we were very suitably located. It was a unique experience for me to have day after day pass without going to school. At first it was a bit of a trial, and when the school bell on the old Jackson School rang, I thought I ought to be out and on my way to Garfield. In fact, I felt that I *must* go. It was hard to think the schools could go on without me.

I spent the days watching the workmen fix up our little home. Many mornings I drove around with Doctor while he was making his calls. Each afternoon I sewed awhile. We rented a piano and that was a source of much pleasure to us both. Miss Chamberlain was a splendid musician and often she would come and play an hour or two for us. I was feeling fine and enjoying everything. One thing gave me some annoyance and a little worry. My hands would get very numb and it was hard for me to do things. (This happened again in 1918-19.)

About four o'clock on the morning of July 22, after a long afternoon and a longer night, we welcomed our baby Karl, with more gladness than we had ever known. We had counted on him and planned for him for such a long time, and now that our hopes were realized, for just a little while it seemed as if there was nothing more to be desired.

Mrs. Lyman, a friend we had made in Holton, came to take care of the baby and me for a few weeks. The summer was a very warm one, and after she went away my troubles began. The baby cried a great deal, both day and night, and what we had thought was prickly heat turned out to be eczema in a very bad form. Every day was a nightmare and the nights were worse. We kept a girl to do the work in the kitchen, and Doctor had a man to take care of the horse and to drive for him.

We felt this was enough trouble for one household, but soon there was to be more. My brother Dave, having finished his college work in Chicago in the spring, had, through Charley's efforts, been invited to come to Topeka to assist Dr. George Pritchard, at that time State Veterinarian. Dave had married on his return to Kansas, so when he came to Topeka in June, he brought Laura with him, and they took rooms on Monroe Street. Laura was a sweet, helpless little body, and I was in no condition to be of very much help to her.

Soon things began to pile up. On October 15, a baby, Hazel, was born to Laura. The winter was very cold—their rooms were not comfortable and

they had not had a chance to make them so. Before
the baby was two weeks old, Dave became seriously
ill with typhoid fever and soon Laura was down
with it, too. She was seriously ill from the first.
We decided to put a bed in our front room and bring
them to our house where we could perhaps take
better care of all of them. This was during the
holidays. Poor Dave was very weak. Baby Hazel
could not get adjusted to the new feeding and was
very fretful. Mother came in to help all she could,
but we had a houseful of trouble.

Day after day Laura grew weaker and weaker;
she was delirious most of the time. She kept repeating, "I want a new coat so I can go home." One
morning when our neighbor and friend, Mr. W. W.
Mills, went by, he stopped to ask how we were getting along and he heard her wail. He told me to come
down to his store and pick out a coat that I thought
she would like. I did, and he sent it up to her with
his best wishes and the hope she would soon be well
enough to wear it. She was delighted with the coat
in her rational moments, and when she died on January 15, 1894, it was on the bed beside her.

Mother, in the great-hearted way that she always
had, put her arms about the motherless little baby
and said she would be its mother. I have often
thought what a cross it was for her to take upon
herself, after all the years of struggle when she had
six of her own and no one to help. Dave went home
with mother and the baby, and after laying his wife
to rest in the little country burial ground near her

childhood home, he came back to his work in Topeka. After a time he married again; his wife had
one child and three children were born of this second marriage. Dave worked with Dr. Pritchard for
many years, dissolving the partnership only a few
years before his death. He died very suddenly, while
he was making a call in the country, on February 14,
1917.

When Karl was three months old, we were happily
surprised one day to receive a telegram saying that
Father and Mother Menninger were coming to pay
us a visit and to see their new grandchild. We were
happy to have them in our new home, and they
spent three joyous weeks with us. The baby was
perfectly satisfactory in every way. Father wanted
to be doing something with him all the time. He insisted that we have a picture taken, and on the day
that Karl was three months old, he carried him up
to the photographer and planned the poses. He
weighed him too, that day, and he weighed 20
pounds. "A fine boy, a fine boy," Father would repeat. One day we drove out to Burnett's Mound and
walked to the top. Grandfather carried the baby
every foot of the way. We ate our lunch on the very
top and talked about the country we could see so
plainly for miles around.

They were happy with us, but we could not keep
them very long. They left a big family Bible as a
souvenir of their visit.

When Karl was able to sit alone, we had a baby

box made for him. We padded it with cotton, covered it with cretonne and put rollers under it. It was a big thing and took up a lot of room, but baby was more important than anything else, so the box always had a place at the sunniest window. That box served for all three of our boys and many people borrowed it. One of the borrowers failed to return it—I have forgotten who it was.

At Christmastime we had a tree for our baby, then six months old. Papa (our home name for Doctor) tried to get his attention centered on one thing or another, but we never could be sure of success. The baby was sitting in his box on Christmas evening surrounded by rattles and other bright baby toys, but he was too young to choose anything. Mr. Blakely came in to bring him a little gift and he put a piece of candy in baby's mouth. Karl licked his lips and smiled, and Mr. Blakely insisted he had drawn the best response from the baby that first Christmas. The great surprise gift was a music box. Doctor told me to sit in the dining room for a few moments while he fixed up one of his packages in the front room. Soon I heard a beautiful tune from that direction. I loved that music box the minute I heard it and I always have loved it. It was used for many years. When it would play no longer, the records and works were sold for brass and the box itself was made into a shoe box.

The winter was a very hard one for all of us. After Laura's death I was exceedingly tired, worried and nervous. One day Mrs. Edward Wilder, who was then very prominent in Topeka, came to call. I had just bathed the baby and had not finished picking up. The one disadvantage of a dear little cottage is that you can see the whole house at once. There was nothing to do but ask her in. Baby cried fretfully and I tried to apologize. Mrs. Wilder said, "Never mind, Mrs. Menninger. I do not think a mother ought ever to apologize about any situation which concerns her children. A mother would understand, nobody else can be expected to. So it is best just to forget it." I have often thought of that advice.

We had some neighbors, the Handys, who always went away for the summer, and one day Mrs. Handy suggested that we move into her big house across the street, for the summer. She thought it would be cooler for us. We accepted her offer and went over, and we were glad to have Mrs. Haynes, a dear woman, move into our cottage. She had been living in a rooming house. In July, her first child, Pauline (now Mrs. Hampton Shirer), was born in the same room where Karl was born. (That little cottage was the birthplace of the first children of six families: the Thompsons, Larimers, Douglases, Hayneses, McClintocks and Menningers.)

On September 1, we moved back from the Handy residence to our own house. The days were still summery, so for our comfort and pleasure Charley put a tent—just a canvas roof on poles—and some outdoor chairs in the back yard. We had only a small patch of ground back of the house—it was seventy-five feet in width and less in length. A walk which

led from the back door to the barn divided the space
unequally. The larger space, to the north, was a
lawn. The fence between us and our neighbors was
brilliant with colorful vines. To hide the front of
the barn, we had erected an arbor and a wisteria vine
was growing over that. South of the walk were roses
—LaFrance and American Beauty, the finest we have
ever had. There were many beautiful annuals, all
flourishing. In the northwest corner we had a pretty
pansy bed. North of the main part of the house was
a bed of lilies of the valley and one of tuberous be-
gonias, most interesting for their gorgeous color,
their beautiful leaves and their great novelty. We all
found it enjoyable and restful to sit out back in the
cool of the evening. Karl was just a little over a year
old; he was interesting and not very much care.

When winter came, Charley felt I should try to
get out among people a little and that we ought to
entertain some of our friends. It was true that we
had not had much social life. Most of my friends
were teaching school, and people thought of me as a
schoolteacher, so I had been rather lonely. But this
fall and winter saw the beginning of my deep friendship with Mrs. George Whitcomb. Through the
years she has had more of my admiration than any
other person I have known. She used to come over
to see me with her baby Philip, who was about nine
months older than Karl, and we would sit and talk,
or push our baby buggies and talk, and I always
enjoyed these hours with her. She had seen much
that I had not seen, and she had a wonderful educa-

tion. With her parents she had traveled extensively abroad, and I had read things her mother, Julia McNair Wright, had written. I felt rich then in knowing Mrs. Whitcomb, and this feeling has never altered.

One evening in early November we decided to have a dinner party for eight—four couples—which was all our room would hold. I prepared everything as well as I could, but with fear and trembling. I do not remember any of the guests except the Whitcombs and McCarters (Margaret Hill, and her husband). Everyone arrived on time but the Doctor. We waited and waited, but finally had to sit down to dinner without him, and the guests went home without seeing him at all. It was very disappointing to me. Three times during the winter we tried to entertain, but Charley was never able to be present.

Chapter 16

MY husband's practice was growing. The telephone was in the bedroom, and it always seemed to ring at the wrong time. The Doctor had to go out at night a great deal, and whenever he was called, the telephone bell would be sure to wake the baby. I would try to soothe him until his father returned; then he was usually more successful in getting him back to sleep. In fact, getting the baby to sleep became the chief problem of our life, and I grew very nervous and fidgety so we decided to rent a larger house. We found a very comfortable old house in Potwin into which we moved in March, 1895. I liked the house and enjoyed roaming about in it and fixing it up as far as we were able. Also, we got a maid named Caroline whom we kept with us quite a while, not for what she really did but for what she meant to do; she was very willing. We enjoyed the winter at Potwin. We had lots of room and plenty of sunshine. Life seemed more worth living.

Besides being busy with his practice, my husband continued to study his medical books assiduously. He has continued to study all his life. Moreover, he early began to gather other physicians together to study with him; he was the leader and virtually the teacher. He began teaching a class of nurses at Christ's Hospital, and he seldom missed a medical meeting, local, state, or national. In the spring of 1895 he attended one of these meetings in Kansas City, and took the baby and me with him. We were invited to stay with a former friend and co-worker in Holton, now Mrs. Abernathy. She had a comfortable home and we had a delightful time. It was the grand opera season, and we heard Wagner's *Parsifal*. The tickets were $5 each, and we sat in the first balcony. For me, this was another wonderful first experience which never lost its flavor.

My husband attended many lectures in the Kansas Medical College and later he was invited to lecture in physiological chemistry and became Professor of Dietetics, and diseases of metabolism. He was especially interested in diabetes mellitus. In 1913, he gave the address to the graduating class and was himself awarded the degree of Doctor of Medicine by the Kansas Medical College, which had become the Medical Department of Washburn College several years before, and which later was taken over by the State University. His earlier degree was from the Chicago Hahnemann Medical College.

Bicycles were much in use those days—the old-fashioned, high-seated kind. Doctor bought one, and it was a great help in making odd calls. It was much easier to get out the "bike" than to harness the horse, hitch him to the buggy, and then undo everything again when he returned. There was a national medi-

cal meeting in Detroit that year and several Kansas
City doctors were taking their bicycles with them to
the convention; they asked Doctor to join them. He
did and reported a great time "seeing Detroit" on a
bicycle. I think it was in this year, 1895, that my
husband joined the Saturday Night Club, the meetings of which he always enjoyed. It was one of his
few recreations in those days, and he continued it for
many years.

In August, 1895, we made a second visit to Charley's parents. We went to St. Louis by train and
then took the boat down the river to Cairo and from
there on up the Ohio and on to Tell City. In a good
many ways it was pleasant but part of the time it
was too warm to be very entertaining. The folks did
not think we should have spent so much of our time
on the way, but we enjoyed it. At the Menningers'
we found Will Kercher, a nephew of Doctor's, who
was then only fourteen and just out of school. Since
he could find no work, Charley thought we ought to
bring him home and send him to school in Topeka.
This we did and Will proved a great help and comfort to me. He made friends quickly and liked to go
to school, and very soon he was quite at home
with us.

On March 18, 1896, a Saturday, as soon as Charley got home, we realized that we must call the nurse
we had engaged, a Mrs. Charters. Will went out
with the surrey to get her. They came back through
a flurry of snow, and it was not long before Edwin
was born. We were looking for a girl, but were

happy to have this chubby, strong, ten-pound boy. Sunday morning the sun shone brightly and, though there was snow on the ground, Will brought in a few dogtooth violets, which he proudly handed to me as an offering in honor of the new baby.

Things went well with the baby and me. We had made up our minds to go back to our little cottage again as soon as baby was old enough. When he was two weeks old, Doctor brought a new phaeton which was quite low, and took me out for a drive. When Edwin was three weeks old we moved back to 1270 Topeka Avenue. The Blakelys were generous in helping us; I took baby to them in his little basket and left him there while we straightened things out in the cottage. Caroline was with us so we were soon settled again.

Edwin was a pretty baby and a great comfort. He was not too heavy, so we enjoyed lifting and handling him. At three months he weighed thirteen pounds. He was good-natured and, unless he got hungry, made us very little trouble. We bought a little hammock and swung it across the corner of the room, and kept him in that until he was nearly a year old. One day I put him in the tiny bedroom and gave him a banana to play with. He was quiet and I thought he was asleep, so I paid no attention to him until perhaps two hours later. Then I found that he had eaten most of the banana, skin and all. I phoned to Doctor and he got quite excited. He immediately gave Edwin ipecac, but with no effect. I think he was expecting some serious trouble, but baby did not show any sign of disorder and was none the worse for the experience.

During the summer we built a window at the south end of the dining room and filled it with flowers. We kept doing something to the little place all the time, and it grew charming and comfortable. Doctor insisted on having a maid after the banana episode, and we tried one after another. Some stayed only a week or two. One of the trials of my life has been trying to get efficient help. I really preferred doing the work myself. One girl we had could go to sleep standing up. She would fall asleep almost as soon as she sat down. She looked perfectly well and was well, she said. Another maid I had, once piled all the china I kept on the sideboard onto the table. She also set the music box on the table. Then she pushed the table around the room so she could clean up. Two of the legs gave out and down went the table and all the dishes, with the music box on top of them. It was a great disaster. Doctor had given me many pieces of pretty china through the years and all of it went down in one crash. I felt wretched about it, but there was nothing to do except to learn a lesson and do the cleaning a better way next time.

It was during this summer that we met Foy Ernest, Mrs. Ehrenfeld's brother. She wrote me about him and said he was in camp here with the boys who were going to the Philippines. We went to the camp and found him. He began visiting us and before the army left we were well acquainted and felt that for his own and his sister's sake we wanted to do all we could for him. After the Kansas unit of the Spanish War forces was disbanded, he stayed with us for four years. He graduated from the Kansas Medical College, then in Topeka, and practiced here for a number of years. He went to France in the World War, remained in the service and is now stationed at the United States Veterans' Psychiatric Hospital, Portland, Oregon.

Mr. and Mrs. Frank Bacon had moved into the little house north of us. Their son Ralph, three months older than Karl, and their daughter Katy, two years older than Ralph, were among my boys' first playmates, as were Isabel and Elizabeth Mills, who lived two doors south. With four children between us and living so close together, Mrs. Bacon and I were kept busy, but Will was a great help.

One winter there was a fad for making fancy lanterns from pasteboard boxes. Everybody made them, but few were as ambitious or successful as the Bacons. When summer came, we strung the lanterns on wires to decorate our front yards, and by fall there was such general interest in the lanterns that an exhibition of them was held in Garfield Park. The Bacons won the first prize. We had some of these lanterns around the place for years afterwards.

In August of 1897, we attended a Chautauqua at Ottawa, Kansas, where we rented a tent. Mr. Bacon and Will drove out in a wagon with the necessary luggage. A day later Mrs. Bacon and I and the children went up by train. It was a very eventful two weeks. We took a little wagon for the baby and Will was great at keeping track of the children when we went to a lecture or did the necessary cooking. Up to that time I had never had any special interest in art, but at this Chautauqua I attended a series of lectures on the "Twelve Masterpieces" and came home enthusiastic to study pictures. For two years I studied hard and every week for a year I wrote a description of a picture; these descriptions were printed by Mrs. Brown in the Holton *Signal*. There was so little interest in the subject in those days that I could borrow as many books from the city library as I wanted and keep them as long as I wanted. Only a few colleges in the country at that time offered a course in art, and it was not easy to get pictures for study purposes.

Near the end of our stay in Ottawa, a bad storm came up. The wind blew a gale, and a large tree fell across our tent, flattening it to the ground. No one was hurt, but the tent was useless. When things calmed down some friends of Mrs. Bacon, who lived in the town, came and took us home with them for the night. The next day we came home on the train.

The storm was not yet over and all the way home the skies were black and threatening. We were glad to get in the house because the wind and rain and hail were fast and furious. One could scarcely see. Even indoors I was apprehensive and the children were badly frightened. I opened the trap door to the cellar and we all went down there. Then it seemed as if the end had come, for suddenly it was all calm.

The clouds had cleared and the sun was shining. We came up to find the big west window broken to pieces; and hailstones covering the front-room carpet and strewn in the dining room and kitchen. It was the worst storm I had ever seen. Thousands of windows were destroyed and many trees were broken down. The hailstones, some of them weighing as much as three-quarters of a pound, covered the ground. The children played ball with them.

About the last of June, 1898, Mrs. J. H. Miller and her son Dwight stopped to see us on their way to a vacation in Pine, Colorado. She had rented a cottage there and urged me to share it with her. I joined her later and for a month things went very well; but the children grew tired of one another and when I found an empty place with two little rooms, we moved in by ourselves. More than a week before we were due to leave, we received a telegram asking us to come home at once. This was near noon and the train left at three. We started to pack at once, gave our stock of supplies to the grocer to dispose of as he liked, sent the trunks to the depot and got down there before train time. But no train came. After a long wait, we were told there would be no train that day, so we could do nothing but go back to the empty house and wait.

When we did get home, there was a great surprise. Doctor told us we were going to have a new home.

Chapter 17

WE bought the big house at 1251 Topeka Avenue on August 22, 1898, and moved into it on October 15. (The cottage was rented for a while, and then we sold it.)

It was very exciting to move into such a big place. We had so little to put into it, but it was a great day for all of us. On our wedding day we had pledged our lives "each for the other and both for God." At that time we had only ourselves, but now we had so much more—two sons, many friends, a beautiful home. I really felt unworthy.

At first most of the rooms were bare, but Christmas brought us a Kimball grand piano for the parlor and the new year brought us an expert pianist. Annie M. Parry Bundy, young, enthusiastic, talented, and just back from studying abroad, came to Topeka to teach music. She stayed with us for three years. She made it a strict rule to practice an hour a day, and we never failed to enjoy her music. I once remarked to Charley, after hearing one of her performances, that nobody's playing pleased me as well as Miss Bundy's, and he replied, "She is an artist; there are not many." Her hearers could not fail to sense how completely she lived her music. After Miss

Bundy left, Myrtie Radcliffe came to study music with Miss Whittlesey, and she had Miss Bundy's room and her place in our home. She practiced six hours a day. She stayed for two years and always delighted us with her playing. I mention these two because music has played an important part in our lives all through the years.

Our new house demanded a special celebration for its first Christmas. It happened that some of our Dickinson County folks had not yet visited us, so we planned a big Christmas party for Howard's family of six, Noble's family of three and mother's family of three. Dave was living here in Topeka. They had all arranged to be here for Christmas Eve and Christ-day Day, and great plans were afoot. We got the biggest tree ever; it reached clear to the ceiling and we decorated it with Christmas ornaments and long strings of popcorn and cranberries. It was finished two days before Christmas so we could have one day to work at the church and one to prepare the necessary food for our guests. We were just about finished when Edwin began to complain. He sneezed and his eyes reddened; when Doctor got home, he was lying down. After one look, Doctor said, "Measles."

It was impossible in those days to telephone or telegraph to the family. They would all be on their way to Abilene by four o'clock in the morning in order to reach Topeka in the afternoon. We finally decided that Uncle Dave must take the eleven o'clock train for Abilene that night. There he had to hire a team and drive fifteen miles out in the country to tell

My Mother at 52; Hazel at 3

My Mother at 75 in Industry, Kansas

them what had happened. He waked up every family except mother's—they were already up, getting ready to start to town. After delivering the bad news, he ate breakfast with mother, drove back to Abilene and was home again in the afternoon. It was a great disappointment which, of course, neither Karl nor Edwin could understand. Part of our Chrismas celebration was packing the boxes of presents to send out to the farms by mail. In spite of disappointments, we had a happy day.

On October 15, 1899, our third baby was born. When Doctor and I were married, we had neither time nor money for the customary wedding rings, so we planned that if we had a daughter, we would celebrate by buying a diamond ring; if we had a son, we would buy a famous painting for the walls of our home. For the third baby, we had chosen the name Clara Louise, sure that it would be a girl. But we had to change our plans. I have never regretted not getting my diamond ring, for we have had a great deal of pleasure through the years from our copies of Bodenhausen's "Madonna," Greuze's "Broken Pitcher" and Corot's "Spring."

Foy Ernest came in with Will to see the baby and me. I said, "Will, the baby is here, but its name is wrong." He answered, "Cut out the Louise and call him Will, after me." And so it was settled—William Claire Menninger.

There never was a more perfect October nor a nicer place for a mother to enjoy her newborn child. Outside my window were large elm trees, yellowed by frost and for days their leaves fell like big drops of colored rain. It was peaceful, restful, beautiful; the whole atmosphere was inspiring and encouraging.

With the coming of William Claire, there were several notable innovations. When Charley started out to be a physician, he began to grow a beard to "add age and dignity," he said; but I might say that lots of young men were doing the same thing. Nobody in Topeka knew him without one. Early in November, he attended a medical meeting and came home with a clean shaven face. It was a real shock to all of us, and we couldn't quite decide what we thought about it. Even good friends did not recognize him at first sight. When people asked him why he did it, he replied, "Most of the doctors at the meeting had clean-shaven faces; the few who didn't were mostly quacks. I chose to be with the doctors." It was quite a while before we grew accustomed to the change.

At this time we began celebrating Thanksgiving by having dinner with the H. A. Kingsley family; one year they would be at our house for dinner and the next year we would go to theirs. On these occasions, the children recited pieces and played their music—Karl and Ethel, the piano; Edwin, the violin; Claire, the cello. And they told us about their schoolwork. We kept up this exchange of Thanksgiving visits until the older children began to feel that they must go to the football game that day. One summer when Mrs. Kingsley was in a hospital,

her husband and three of their children spent six
weeks with us; we felt that these friends were almost
part of the family.

Mother Knisely visited us that Christmas and
with a new home and a new boy and Christmas
altogether, we felt we really had something to interest her. We took her downtown to see Santa
Claus, and on Christmas Eve she saw him again at
the church, where he gave all the children little red
bags of candy. We played the music box while Santa
handed out gifts. I think mother was thrilled by the
occasion but she did not want to stay long. She had
always lived in the country, and she did not like the
town with its crowds and noise. Before she left she
said to me, "If anything should happen to Leah
before my time to go, won't you get someone among
the old friends to come and care for me? I would be
so unhappy here." I promised. Leah, Howard and I
were all with her in the old Industry home when she
peacefully fell asleep twenty years later, in December, 1919, a few days after her seventy-seventh
birthday.

In 1901 we attended the Pan-American Exposition in Buffalo, New York—just Charley and I. We
left Claire with the Kingsleys and Karl, Edwin
and Hiram (Kingsley) spent a whole month with
mother, Aunt Leah and Hazel on the farm. The
American Medical Association held its annual meeting at Richfield Springs, New York, that year, and
after attending all the sessions, we went on to the
Fair at Buffalo. As this was my first experience of

this kind, I found everything extremely interesting. After Buffalo we visited the old Pennsylvania home and spent two days with Uncle Rell and his family.

We took the train to Gettysburg, on the Fourth of July, a very warm day. After dinner at a place near the cemetery, we drove around the battlefield to see the most famous monuments and listened to the stories the guide told at historic sites. There were very few people on the grounds and we did not hear a single firecracker all day long. It was the quietest Fourth of July we ever spent. Personally, I did not feel that I had gained much from the visit. I came away feeling that the time mother held me in her arms and looked into President Lincoln's face was the best of my three visits to Gettysburg.

At the Fair, Doctor had been fascinated by the new Apollo piano players and had ordered one. It soon arrived and for a long time had a prominent place in front of our piano. It was rolled back and forth every day for several years, for somebody had to have the keyboard for piano practice. When Doctor had time, he played the Apollo. While Miss Bundy was with us we had a musical once a month, from September to June. These were most interesting occasions and very popular. We could accommodate one hundred people; we bought folding chairs and kept them stacked in the back hall. Sometimes I helped out with a talk on pictures and a number of amateur performers also entertained us.

This was also the summer we first used a sleeping porch. I had observed that the children slept better outdoors than they did indoors. We put a railing around the roof of the back porch and kept the children out all night. Doctor and I tried this ourselves and liked it; so we built a sleeping porch big enough to accommodate the whole family. It was the very first one in Topeka, but they soon became popular and were added to many old homes and built into new ones.

Mother Menninger's fatal illness in March, 1902, took Doctor back to the old Tell City home. Edwin went with him for company. It was his first train ride and he thoroughly enjoyed himself. A few days after his return, however, he was taken sick with scarlet fever. He was ill several days; then William Claire took the disease, and was seriously ill. For one whole week Doctor stayed home in quarantine with me. For most of that time, the doctors had little hope that we could save William Claire. When he began to improve, Edwin was getting around and soon Claire was able to be up also. We stayed upstairs for six long weeks, while Foy Ernest lived downstairs with Karl. He prepared our meals and put the trays on the back stairs for us to pick up. During the latter weeks, Doctor stayed at the office nights and days. We visited with him through the upstairs window. After the anxiety had passed, I found quarantine interesting. It gave me an opportunity for a searching of self such as I never had before, and there were helpful results which have continued through the years.

Mr. Hugh U. Mudge, General Manager of the

Santa Fe Railroad, and his family were our next door neighbors. In late July, Mrs. Mudge called me over for a front-porch visit. She told me they were about to leave for their annual vacation of a month in the Pecos Mountains near Glorietta, New Mexico. The woman she had engaged to do the cooking had suddenly been taken ill and she did not know where to find anyone to take her place. Sympathetically, I said, "I wish I could go and do it for you!" "Would you go?" she asked. "I surely would," I replied, "but what could I do with my baby?" "Take him along," she answered. Doctor urged me to go with her, as the two older boys were out on the farm with mother. A few days later we were on our way. It was such fun to ride in Mr. Mudge's private car with the family and to know that just back of it was a personal baggage car with everything required for the entire family for a whole month, including a dog and a pony! Claire and I had our own tent. I did all the cooking for from six to ten people, but there was plenty of time to enjoy myself. Mr. Mudge hired several horses and there was a colored man to help tend them, to get in the wood for big bonfires every night and to clean the fish which were caught every other day. Between fishing days they rode up and down the mountains, and sometimes I was able to go. We baked our bread in covered Dutch ovens among the hot coals of a big outdoor fire. Claire was supremely happy playing about the camp with the dog. Mr. Mudge made a pretty little chair for him that we brought with us when we came home the last of August.

Just before Christmas of that year, Mr. Mudge got a new private car for his personal use, and Mrs. Mudge dedicated it by inviting two other friends and me to go with her to Chicago to see the window decorations. There were just the four of us, and a cook and waiter, traveling in grand style. We started out happily, but at Chicago I was so car sick that I had to stay in bed and I suffered a great deal coming home. Mrs. Mudge would have given me many trips on the Santa Fe lines if I had not found traveling so uncomfortable.

Chapter 18

MANY wonderful things came to us in 1903. Early in February, I happened to look through the window and saw a boy tying a little pony to our hitching post. He put his arms about the pony's neck for a moment, then hurried away. Doctor had bought the pony for our boys; the former owner was going away to college and had to part with it. The pony's name was Ruth. Edwin took possession of her at once and always seemed to be her master. He liked to do errands. Soon after she came to us, I sent him on an errand not very far from home, and I suggested that he take Claire with him. They started off all right, both of them sitting properly on the buggy seat, but when Edwin came back there was no baby.

Just then the telephone rang and a woman's voice said, "Mrs. Menninger, do you know where your baby is?" It was a neighbor, a block away, and she went on, "I have him in the house, but he is hurt." I rushed down, got him and brought him home. His little face was all bruised and his nose was bleeding, but he wasn't seriously hurt. He had fallen out on the pavement when the buggy jounced over the streetcar tracks. Edwin didn't even see him fall. We found a safer, two-seated little red wagon for the pony to draw; it could carry the whole family. Ruth served us for five years; she was twenty-seven years old when she died.

In March we got our stereopticon! We wired the dining room, put a curtain over the double doors between the dining room and the sitting room, and started to show the illuminated pictures. They are still going strong! My slides have been used many times at home, church and school, and they have been sent out by mail to instruct and entertain people in other cities.

That same month Doctor sent Mother and Leah two hundred apple trees and two hundred grapevines to plant on her farm. This was one of several attempts to help plant things on the farm, but the result has never been lasting or encouraging. Hot winds, drouth, bugs of all kinds, grasshoppers, army worms, blight and sometimes late frosts—all these are and have long been enemies of the Kansas farmer. We have experienced them all, some of them many times.

Decoration Day opened with a drizzling rain which turned into a downpour and a flood. At about four o'clock, Doctor telephoned me. "The rain is terrible," he said. "Everything is being flooded. Plan a supper for seventeen people—we'll have to take care of them. Order ham and flour and all the groceries you can. I don't know when I'll be able to get home."

Doctor's estimate of the people we would have to care for was too low. It is almost impossible to describe the terrible results of that flood. For one whole week we housed and fed thirty people, and for two weeks we conducted a hospital for more than twenty. There were twenty-three children; measles broke out and several were quite ill. Their fathers left, but four mothers stayed. Doctor lived at the office. We had a colored boy, Frank Preer, who helped me. Mrs. C. G. Blakely, Mr. W. W. Mills and a score of my Bible Class women did what they could to furnish clothing and bedding and to take care of many other needs, for these flood victims had lost everything they owned. The whole episode was a nightmare, and I don't know how we managed to do all we did.

The outstanding event of 1904 was a week at the St. Louis Exposition with Karl and Edwin and Sadie Dunn, the office girl. I remember vividly how Doctor tried to interest the boys in the different things there were to see—and how urgently the boys preferred their own way of seeing things. Each of the boys wore a very dark blue flannel blouse and a red Windsor tie. You can never guess how fortunate it was that we had chosen that particular color combination, for whenever the boys got too far away from us, we could spot the glowing red on the dark blue and go after them.

My husband's love of nature and flowers soon made our back yard a very beautiful spot. It was landscaped and carefully planted and tended. He loved passionately everything connected with it, called every flower by name and enjoyed introducing them to his friends. He spent as much time as he could adding to the beauty of the garden, and he liked to rest there after his hard, demanding work. His particular hobby was peonies. The first fall we were at 1251 Topeka Avenue, he planted six roots on the north line of our property. The next fall, he put fifty more at the far end of the lots south of the barn. The third year saw a row of peonies along the south line of our property. And there were many other flowers, of course.

But with three boys growing up rapidly and needing a place to play—especially to play baseball —it became increasingly difficult to raise flowers. There were no playgrounds in the parks in those days, and when they played near the house, the ball often found its way into the flower beds and the boys went after it. The flowers were never the same after they came out, and when Doctor got home and discovered the damage, he was naturally displeased and discouraged.

Something had to be done, so we finally gave all the plants but the peonies to Christ's Hospital and made a playground of the back yard. My husband then bought three lots at the corner of Plass Avenue and 17th Street, put a wire fence around them and made his flower garden there. Peonies predominated, and it was not long before they began to bloom and to attract attention and comment. They were really a marvelous sight. One year, just before Decoration Day, the garden was robbed of many of its blooms and badly spoiled. For two years after that, we kept a watchman on duty before Decoration Day.

Many people wanted to buy the flowers, but Doctor could not bear to sell them. He loved to show the flowers to his friends and give them a bouquet—but *sell* them! It was not until 1919 that he gave Pearl and me permission to sell what we could from the garden on Decoration Day. He wouldn't even watch us, and when I told him in the evening that we had sold over 100 dozen, he was sure the garden was ruined. We went out together the next morning so he could see for himself that it was still blazing with color.

After that we sold peonies from the Plass garden until we moved to Oakwood in 1923. We began transferring them to the new home in August of that year and planted more until we had several acres. The year they were at their best we cut over 2,000 dozen and sold every one. Doctor grew the first peonies that Topeka had. Today everyone has a few, and now they are shipped from Topeka by the carload.

When the flowers had been taken out of the back yard, we put up a high wire screen on the north and south to protect the neighboring gardens and turned the spot over to the boys. It soon became a gathering place where they played ball, put up tents for camping out all night and generally had a good time in complete safety. I had a full view of the yard from my kitchen window.

For several years, we could always find a group of boys there day or night, during good weather. There was always one tent, usually two and sometimes four. They all got along well, and if there was any trouble I could usually settle it merely by looking out the window. I feel that those were happy and worthwhile days that some of the boys will never forget. The playground gave them a chance to do things for themselves and by themselves.

The boys never tired of going to their grandmother's during their summer vacations, and it was a splendid thing for them. There were so many enjoyable privileges in the country which they did not have in town. Then, too, there were interesting little jobs for them to do which added zest to everything because they felt they were being useful. Doctor and I always went to see them on the Fourth of July and brought them a satchel full of fireworks.

Edwin and Claire had bicycles, and when Edwin was about twelve, they wanted to ride out to their grandmother's. The distance was a hundred miles, and there were no paved roads at that time. Victor Blakely decided to join them. The three boys were fitted out with proper clothing, given some money and a little baggage, and they started out. They rode as far as St. Mary's the first afternoon, to Chapman the second night and finished the trip the next day. After they had started, I felt very uneasy and I was sorry we had let them go. But Doctor said they

would be all right, and they were, but it did seem
to me an unnecessarily severe journey for children
so young—Claire was only eight and Victor ten.
They had a good time and after a week with grandmother they rode back as far as Wamego where a
broken chain made them glad to come the rest of the
way by train. I am sure they have always enjoyed
recalling this adventure.

The last year that all of them went to the country
was 1907. I had been to Winona Lake, Indiana,
to attend some Bible classes and I found everything
so interesting and helpful that the next year I took
the two older boys with me. They were very happy
there and found something interesting to do every
minute. Claire was out at his grandmother's, but he
was not happy there without his brothers, so Doctor
sent him and Minna Koester to me at Winona Lake
for the rest of the season, and Claire had a fine time.
We each had a definite program to follow from nine
to twelve in the morning. I attended Bible classes,
Karl went to a nature study class, and Edwin and
Claire to a boys' club that kept them busy and interested with games and the like. I hurried home before the boys and had dinner ready for them.

One summer Mrs. Blakely and her two boys ac-
companied us to Winona Lake. Claire stayed at her
cottage with Victor, and Charles was with us. The
two fathers spent a week with us. They had some
fine sport—they swam and fished and boated and
hiked and were boys with the boys.

The gatherings at Winona Lake gave us a rare opportunity to meet many fine people. We talked with Schumann-Heink and her son, and with Billy Sunday, Edwin's idol. Billy Sunday's home was at Winona Lake and the great Wilbur Chapman had a beautiful cottage there. E. O. Excell was leader of music. The New York Symphony Orchestra was there for a week and gave two concerts a day. There were some excellent bands and many helpful speakers to inspire and entertain us. Governor Hoch of Kansas came to lecture and he was gracious enough to take dinner with us in our cottage; we saw him off at the train afterward. During the last two years we went there, I taught a Bible class for an hour a day.

We loved it all, and the time we spent there was most helpful to the boys and to me. We were sorry about Doctor—all alone in that big, empty house, but we tried to help by sending him a letter every day, each one writing his own story. I know that Doctor enjoyed those letters.

My son William Claire has refreshed my memory about the Boy Scout activities which formed an important influence in our home over a period of several years. As I have explained, the neighborhood boys used to pitch tents in our back yard and sleep there—sometimes as many as fifteen of them. When the Boy Scout movement began—first as the American Boy Scouts—this group formed a natural nucleus and the boys organized as Scouts about 1910.

Very shortly after the inception of this association, however, the Boy Scouts of America was started and they transferred to that, becoming Troop Two, under the direction of Ralph Searle, in 1911. In March, 1912, twelve of the boys, including William Claire, passed their Tenderfoot tests.

In the fall of 1912, Mr. Harry I. Woods, then Professor of Astronomy at Washburn College, became Scoutmaster of the group, but the next spring, the group then active found itself without a leader and I was pressed into service to hold the little Patrol together. At their request, I met with them each week at their Patrol meeting, which was held in William Claire's room. In the summer of 1913, the first city-wide Boy Scout Camp was held and two of the boys from our group, Edwin Nellis and William Claire, went to the Camp, which was run by Rev. John H. Fazel, one of the pioneers in Scouting in Topeka. When they returned in the fall, Mr. Fazel became Scoutmaster, and the group grew to twenty or twenty-five boys, meeting in the "club room" of our home every Friday night.

Mr. Fazel was succeeded in the spring of 1914 by Mr. P. F. Schilling, known to the boys as Zeke. The following year the Troop moved down to its permanent headquarters at the First Presbyterian Church. As time went on, William Claire became Scoutmaster and later organized a Sea-Scout unit which was three times awarded first place in competition with "Ships" in cities all over the country.

Now Will's sons are in this Troop, and their father is on the National Executive Board of Scouting, and he is the author of a *Handbook for Sea-Scout Leaders*.

Chapter 19

ALL at once, in 1910, things changed radically. We bought a new Cadillac car; Karl graduated from high school and entered Washburn College; and my Bible classes voted a hundred dollars for me to attend the International Sunday School Convention in Washington that year. To this Convention the Sunday school sent Mrs. Estey, who had been Superintendent for some years; Dr. and Mrs. Crumbine; Mrs. Ames, a banker's wife; Mr. J. H. Engel, State Sunday School Secretary; and Mrs. Frank Bacon.

Mrs. Charles Curtis, the Senator's wife, met us at the depot in Washington. She had asked me to be her guest, and I was delighted. I shared a room with Dolly, Senator Curtis' sister, for the whole week. Mrs. Curtis drove me somewhere every day in her electric car. Dolly showed me the White House and introduced me to President Taft in his private office. We visited the Senate and the House of Representatives in session. Senator Curtis took me for a ride in the little car that runs underground between the two houses and saves many steps for those working there.

The last evening of our stay they gave a dinner for all the Topekans. There were twelve at the table, and it was all so wonderful to me—the linen, the dishes, the food and the way it was served. We all felt that we had been greatly honored, and we were most appreciative of all the courtesies they showed us. Senator and Mrs. Curtis gave me a souvenir—a copy of *The Life and Morals of Jesus of Nazareth*, by Thomas Jefferson, printed in 1904 by the Government Printing Office.

In 1910, my three sons formed "a partnership," the Kawceam Stamp Company, a name made up from their initials. Everyone in the neighborhood was interested in it. They did not learn a great many definite facts from their study of stamps, but they grew familiar with the names of countries and their locations. All the boys still collect stamps.

In 1912, we drove to Colorado for a month, and experienced all the inconveniences that went with overland trips in those early days—flat tires, bad roads, no markers, no camping places, no eating places. Automobile travel in those days featured open cars, linen dusters, long flowing veils, muddy roads and general discomfort. The poorest of present-day gravel roads would have been welcomed then. There were a few hard surfaced roads, but farmers were disapprovingly discussing the effect they had on horses' feet.

In high school Edwin belonged to a group of boys called the Stags. They wanted to hold regular meetings outside of school hours but it was hard to find a meeting place. Edwin suggested that we set aside a room downstairs in our home as a kind of clubroom where they could hold their meetings. This room was about fifteen by fifteen, with a ten-foot ceiling; it had three large windows, a fireplace and one door that opened directly into the front hall. We furnished it with chairs, books and games and it became the boys' clubroom. Through the years, the boys came and went as they liked; three rings of the doorbell announced someone for the clubroom. The boys had their meetings, read and played games and had a good time generally, but they were not allowed to smoke nor indulge in any roughhouse. The grownups would be somewhere around the house but never in the room with them. Edwin usually kept fruit in the room, and now and then there was a surprise of ice cream, homemade chocolate candy or pumpkin pie with whipped cream. This last was always the favorite. After high school Edwin went to Washburn, but the downstairs room was still reserved for the boys.

Next the Alpha Delta fraternity group absorbed our interest and there are many happy and amusing memories of those days. When the fraternity set up its own house, I made curtains for the windows, and they "borrowed" chairs, pots, kettles, pans and other things they needed. One day they invited me to dinner and said they were adopting me as Mother of the fraternity. Every year for six or seven years, they invited me out on Mother's Day.

Occasionally when some of the boys got too far away from home after a late date, we provided beds for them. Once a year we served dinner on the back porch for the current group of boys.

Doctor was operated upon twice in 1914, and it was late fall before he was completely well. Karl went back to Wisconsin, Edwin to Washburn, Claire to high school. Charley Menninger, who had been living with us for two years, married Agda Hassing and moved to a home of his own.

Edwin entered the School of Journalism at Columbia University in the fall of 1916. At the end of the year, he came home and worked for Charles S. Gleed on the Kansas City *Journal,* returning to Columbia the following winter. Before the end of the year, he began to work nights on the New York *Tribune.*

On September 1, 1916 Karl married Grace Gaines. The wedding took place at Grace's home, 1524 Topeka Avenue. Immediately afterwards they took the train for Boston where Karl was to finish his last year at Harvard Medical School. Then in May 1917, Doctor and I went East, spending a few days at Columbia University with Edwin, and then going on to Boston for Karl's graduation. This ceremony in a great university was a new experience for me. The gowned leaders and graduates were very interesting and imposing, but the whole thing was so formal and impersonal that I did not get the satisfaction I should like to have had from the occasion. We spent a week seeing Boston and enjoying a visit with Karl and Grace in their little apartment in Belmont. The things I remember most vividly about Boston

are Sargent's "Frieze of the Prophets" in the public
library, the homes of some of the famous men whose
names and books we knew, Bunker Hill Monument,
the Arnold Arboretum, and a fish dinner in a restaurant down by the ocean. The four of us went
home to Kansas together.

Karl took care of his father's office for a month
while Doctor and I went to Chicago to attend a
medical meeting. We came home by way of Tell
City to see the Menninger families.

While we were away, an accident with a runaway
team had taken my brother Howard to the hospital
with a badly hurt ankle and it seemed necessary to
amputate his foot. But an operation was performed
that saved the foot and, although it is not as good
as new, it is much better than none.

At that same time one of my Bible Class students
and helpers, Pearl May Boam, had been taken to the
hospital for an appendix operation and she had the
room next to Howard. They were two very discouraged people, so neither of them made good progress.
Some weeks after Pearl returned to her home, Doctor
said that she could get up if we could only make
her believe that she could. So on a Sunday evening
a few days later, we took her for a ride and then
parked on the east side of the State House steps to
hear a sermon. Then we took her home with us and
kept her for the night. The next morning we urged
her to stay with us. We told her we needed her and
we felt she needed us; and so it turned out. She did

stay and she has been a comfort and a good daughter to both of us ever since.

In February, 1919, Karl and Grace came to Topeka from Boston to make their home. Karl and his father agreed to form a partnership and work together. In March, they moved from 727 Kansas Avenue, where Doctor's office had been for twenty-nine years, to more spacious and modern quarters in the Mulvane Building. Mamie Johnson, the office girl for many years, stayed with them. A little later Dr. Netherton, Mildred Law, John Stone, Mary Sholund and Ingeborg Lindquist joined them.

Edwin gave up his work at the University and for six years he was assistant and then cable editor of the *Tribune*. He married Ella Waldron and lived in Jackson Heights, Long Island, when his first child, Edwin, Jr., was born on October 26, 1921. The work on the *Tribune* was extremely interesting. Edwin learned a great deal from it, and with his warm, genial disposition he made many friends.

It was night work, however, and very strenuous. So when he heard of an opportunity at West Palm Beach, Florida, he and his wife moved there in September 1922. After some months on the staff of the Palm Beach *Post,* he bought a weekly newspaper known as the South Florida *Developer,* and moved it and his family to Stuart, Florida, where he became very active. Largely as the result of his efforts and the assistance of Karl's father-in-law, Mr. H. N. Gaines, a new county was split off from Palm Beach

County in 1926, and Stuart became its county seat. In 1928 Edwin married Mrs. Patsy Underhill Estelle.

In June, 1919, we prevailed on Claire to drive us to California for a vacation. Dr. and Mrs. Magee, Dr. and Mrs. Crumbine and Violet, Mr. and Mrs. O. E. Walker and Mrs. Fred Derby were all in Long Beach, and we planned to join them. The drive across the western plains and the mountains was very interesting and beautiful. I think the petrified forest was of more interest to us than anything else. We spent two days at the Grand Canyon. The roads were not always good and rain gave us some trying experiences. We carried our own tent and camped by the wayside at night.

At Long Beach we rented an apartment and put in the days, but nobody seemed to be much interested in anything. We visited with the folks at times, slept, read and somehow got through the vacation. William Claire was too full of his future plans and ambitions in New York to enjoy lolling around in California, and Doctor's heart was with Karl and his work in Topeka. Both were very restless, so they set an early date to return by rail. The very day they planned to leave a strike was called and they had to stay a week longer.

Pearl and I stayed until September, and returned by train. On the whole, it seemed as if we had wasted our time. I think we all like best to have some definite purpose in the things we do, including vaca-

My Husband and I, 1912 and 1939

tions. I was not happy with nothing to do but eat, sleep and have a good time.

Now that so many of our interests in the house at 1251 had changed—with the boys grown up and away from home—we talked about the possibility of renting or selling the house. But all this was rather vague and we had reached no decision at all. However, a few days after we got home from California, the telephone rang and a woman's voice asked, "Is your home for sale?"

The would-be purchaser came over that same day to look at the house, and on September 15 we sold it with practically all the furniture that had accumulated through the twenty-one years we lived there. It was nice that the sale came about so naturally and easily. If I had had time to ponder the memories that filled every corner from garret to cellar, I couldn't have given up the house.

We had to find a place only for Doctor, Pearl and myself; and this was very adequately provided by Pearl's old homestead at 1411 West Tenth Street. We lived there until September, 1923. It was quite comfortable and required little housework. The one drawback was that there was insufficient room for the practice of my husband's hobby of gardening.

This stay in Pearl's old home was a sort of adjusting period that was good for all of us. William Claire had gone to college in New York; Karl and Grace and baby Julia had moved into a little home in Auburndale; Edwin was in Florida; and we lived very quietly. I undertook the weekly job of gathering up a number of blind people in my car (seven in all) and taking them to the Y.W.C.A. where they spent the afternoons under the guidance of a leader who taught them how to weave baskets and mats.

Somewhat later a new experience came to us through Mr. H. W. Jones, principal of Branner School. He asked Pearl if she would like to help in the kindergarten. He knew her fondness for children and felt sure she would make good. We decided that she and I would drive to Chicago and spend six weeks in the kindergarten training school. At the end of the term Doctor came to Chicago and drove back with us. Pearl took up kindergarten teaching at once in the Branner School, the one in which I taught when I first came to Topeka.

Doctor and I had always planned to live in the country someday. We were continually selecting this or that spot for our home, and whenever the question would arise to keeping or discarding anything, we always asked ourselves whether we could use it in our ideal country home. Now we were thinking seriously about this country place. Every time we saw a pretty little shaded home along the wayside we became more interested than ever in living in the country. But when we investigated, we would usually find that the house had no water, or no electricity—and we realized that when it rained we would have to contend with the mud. These things often put a damper on our enthusiasm for a time, but never for very long.

In 1922, Mr. and Mrs. A. A. Goddard invited us to come out and sit with them for an evening's chat. They lived north of town in a charming little house which they used only in the summer. It was so entrancing that Doctor asked Mr. Goddard if he wouldn't sell us a plot of his land for a building site. But he wouldn't think of it! "Well," said Doctor as we left, "I wish you would promise to give me the first chance to buy if you ever want to sell." Mr. Goddard agreed, and a few months later he did decide to sell his entire place.

Our decision was made in May, but we did not get possession until September. Through the summer we spent many evenings parked on the roadside near our new home, planning what we would do when we lived there. We moved to Oakwood on Saturday, September 15, 1923, and wanted to be settled before William Claire left for New York. Pearl May went out to the new home early, with Richard, the colored man. I stayed at Pearl's home to see the things loaded. When I got out there at six in the evening, the table was set for supper, the curtains were up, there was a fire in the grate, every piece of furniture was in place, and everything was inviting and restful.

We were very happy as we ate our first meal and watched the lighted city from our table. As we sat talking of the new things that had come to us, a message came from Edwin in Palm Beach. "Barbara

Menninger born tonight. Mother and daughter doing well!" This was our fourth grandchild—Julia,
Edwin, Jr., Robert, Barbara.

William Claire had come out with us and he slept
here one night—his last in our home. He went on
then to Cornell Medical School where he graduated
in 1924. After an interneship in Bellevue Hospital,
he declined invitations to remain in New York and
returned to practice in Topeka with his father and
brother, bringing his new bride, who was Catharine
Wright of East Orange, New Jersey.

Karl and Will, in partnership with their father,
worked toward the development of a clinic. This
grew out of Doctor's long expressed admiration for
group practice as exemplified by the Mayo Clinic,
with its high standards of efficiency and progressive-
ness.

Daddy has always been a devoted husband and
a loving indulgent father to his boys. I could ask
no greater gift for them than that they might be
like him in spirit and in purpose toward those they
love. My dream was for a husband who would be
tall and slender, intelligent, and interesting—and I
had hoped we would like the same things. My
dreams have been fulfilled beyond anything I could
have desired. He is still a student, always ready to
discuss almost anything, and he is still a teacher.
His wonderful memory has been a great help to him,
for he has always been able to remember people and
to call them by name.

Chapter 20

RELIGION was an accepted part of my life as a child. Everybody I knew went to church and Sabbath school. Here, for rewards of little blue tickets, they committed verses of Scripture to memory. These blue tickets were exchanged for red ones which in turn were exchanged for a coveted prize of some kind—usually a Bible. I earned my first Bible by memorizing the Psalms. It had a black leather binding with gold clasps and trimming.

At home, the Bible was read morning and night and there were few other books to be had. However, there was no one to give me very much information about the Bible stories. I read about Saul, the first King of Israel, and Saul stricken to the earth on his way to Damascus, and naturally I wondered how one story connected with the other. Grandmother couldn't help me, and grandfather was likely to say, "You'd better just read about Jesus." (I have often thought since that this was not such bad advice.)

Later, it was part of my weekly program to teach in Sunday School, and I usually taught in the Primary Department. But I was always eager to know the Bible better. In the fall of 1897, I learned that our pastor's wife, who conducted a Bible class for unmarried young women, had discovered a new book, Blakeslee's *Outlines,* which included a course of connected study through the Bible. I was jubilant when she said I could attend the class, and I planned to give up teaching the Bible in Sunday School until I had studied it through.

I was on hand for the class the following Sunday, and I brought a friend or two who were just as much interested as I. We were all pleased with the introductory lesson and looked forward to the coming Sabbaths with great anticipation. But it was not to be. One day that week, our pastor, Dr. Countermine and Mrs. Countermine, called on me to say that the girls—most of them as old as I—said they wouldn't mind having me attend, but they could not have married women in their class.

Dr. Countermine and my husband discussed the matter and finally suggested that I take my "old married women" and organize a class of my own to study through the Bible. This seemed too much to undertake, but I wanted so much to study the Bible that the temptation was great. The thought stayed in my heart and mind.

In November we were holding a series of afternoon prayer meetings in the church parlor, and one day the question was raised about the answering of prayers. At that moment the door opened and Mrs. J. W. F. Hughes came into the room and the thought flashed through my mind—I will ask Mrs. Hughes if she would join a Bible class if we organize one; if she says yes, I'll take it as an answer to my prayers whether to lead the Bible class. The moment we were dismissed I hurried over to Mrs. Hughes. "I know we have never spoken before," I said, "but I want to ask you if you would join a class to study through the Bible if we organize one."

"It is just the thing I have wanted to do for years!" she replied enthusiastically. We sat down together and made a few plans for starting a mixed class, the members of which agreed to act as supply teachers in the Sabbath school. We secured the coveted Blakeslee's *Outlines* and started our work in January, 1898. For a year we held our meetings in the back of the church, then for several months we met in the church kitchen, but this arrangement was not satisfactory, so we dismissed the class in May and planned to meet again in the fall.

When William Claire was three weeks old, we had our first fall meeting in the church parlor; thirty women were present. After that we met regularly on Monday afternoons. At the end of the first year there was so much interest in the study that we started a second class, which met on Tuesday afternoons, with an enrollment of seventy.

It was during the second year of the Bible class that I spent the month of August with the Mudges in New Mexico. Near the end of my vacation, I received three letters from women in my Monday class, and every one of them asked, in one way or another, why we didn't have prayer at our meetings. My first reaction was to wonder why I had not thought of this myself. But then I reflected that our only purpose in meeting was to study the Bible and I had never thought of adding anything to that. But I found it difficult to forget the suggestion and I went home assuring myself that there was no reason why we should not include prayer in our meetings, although I was somewhat uneasy about it.

I had made up my mind to open the next Monday class with a prayer. I had the words all ready, but when the time came, I just could not get them out. The next week was no better, and by this time I was really miserable over my failure. Just before I started for the church the next week, I asked God to help me conquer this strange embarrassment, and when I stood before the class, I managed to get through a short prayer. I have no recollection of the words. I announced that beginning with the next week, a class member would be assigned to open each meeting with prayer. Mrs. A. K. Rodgers then rose quietly in her place and said, "Girls, you know how some of us have prayed every day for a year for this precious hour; now let us give thanks for an answered prayer."

It is impractical to list the entire membership of my classes, much as I should like to do so, but for sentimental reasons I want to record the names of the members of that first class, the Old Monday Bible Class (1899-1903). They were:

Mrs. W. A. Quigley	Mrs. R. S. Magee
Mrs. A. K. Rodgers	Mrs. J. W. F. Hughes
Mrs. W. M. Davidson	Mrs. L. H. Strickler

Mrs. J. F. Brown   Miss Hattie Drake
Mrs. E. G. Foster   Mrs. E. J. Whittaker
Mrs. R. E. Hawkins   Mrs. Jas. D. Walker
Mrs. J. E. Moon   Mrs. M. M. Phelps
Mrs. W. B. Whitton   Mrs. T. S. Stevens
Mrs. M. E. Holmes   Mrs. Hattie Heaton
Mrs. F. E. Grote   Mrs. Jeanette Thomas
Mrs. H. W. Jones   Mrs. L. B. McClintock
Mrs. D. Q. Diven   Mrs. G. F. Worley
Mrs. D. H. Scott   Mrs. M.M. Miller
Mrs. C. T. Trapp

The Monday class—28 of us—finished the four year course in 1903. In token of our completion of the work, we hung a large picture of the Transfiguration in our church study room. The class was so enthusiastic about the way I had helped them study the Bible that they urged me to expand the work in every way possible. The group pledged itself to act as my board or council, and for twenty years they met every fall to discuss plans for the coming year.

During May and June of 1903, the Y.W.C.A. and the Topeka churches conducted a six-weeks course in Bible study under the direction of Miss Grace Saxe. It was a well-organized project and everything went smoothly. Miss Saxe stayed at our home and she was a great inspiration to me. When her work was finished, my two classes (78 members) gave a party for her at our home. We had a fine program, and when the party was over, my classes gave me enough ten dollar gold pieces to enable me to go to Chicago with Miss Saxe and spend a week in the Moody Bible Institute. I still remember the help and encouragement that week gave me in my later teaching.

About this time I found myself becoming more and more dissatisfied with the Blakeslee *Outlines*. There seemed to be so much preliminary work that had little connection with the Bible itself. Another difficulty was that we had no money. Each member paid for her own books, but that was all. I discussed the matter with my husband and he said, "I don't mind helping you get things for your Bible class, but I do think that if you can't persuade the women that they are getting enough out of it to make them willing to help to get the material you need, you'd better quit." I was puzzled about what to do, but I certainly did not want to quit.

In August I went back to the mountains again. My mother took all three of the children so I had plenty of time to think. I had been making a few revisions in the outlines to improve them for our purposes, but it became plainer all the time that what I really needed was an outline of every book of the Bible, with every question directed to the Bible itself. One day, after the noon meal was finished, I went to a place I called my own, under a big, spreading tree and sat on the ground with my books in my lap.

Everything was very quiet, and after a little while I opened my Bible and before I left the spot I had outlined roughly the entire Book of Genesis. That

evening after the campfire had burned low and the
tents were all dark, I continued to work alone at
an improvised table of orange boxes, my only light
a tallow candle. The morning sun lighted the eastern sky and crept over the treetops before I closed
my books. What a thrilling night it had been! Six
sheets of paper reposed in my Bible, and the rough
sketch of Genesis had been transformed into a finished one. I was sure then that I could do the same
thing with every book of the Bible.

I went home eager to tell the council my plans
for the next year. But when I announced that I intended to make up my own questions for each lesson,
and that I would charge $5 a year for the course,
they were opposed to both plans. Some of them felt
that there might be something to say for the new
outlines, but on the whole they thought it would
be better to stick to the books we knew. As for paying $5 to belong to a Bible class, it was simply un-
heard of. They told me that such revolutionary ideas
would ruin my chances for getting together any class
at all.

But I refused to be dissuaded. "If I teach again,"
I said, "it's going to be with my own outlines and
that requires some working capital." They remained
obdurate, but I was not discouraged. That meeting
was held on a Thursday afternoon, and on Saturday
evening the *State Journal* carried an announcement
to the effect that I would be at home every afternoon
of the following week to enroll anyone interested in
the week-day Bible study class. The Sunday morn-

ing *Capital* carried the same announcement. At the end of the week, 112 women had enrolled, including several members of the old class, and on the first Monday of October, 1903, we started another Monday Bible class, which was to follow the new plan. Before the close of the year, the enrollment had reached 198. In May, 1904, the Tuesday class had closed with public graduation exercises. Fifty completed the four years' work, and every year there were and are graduates—sometimes more than 100. The largest number enrolled in any one year up to 1919 was 400.

In 1923, Mrs. E. C. Seger conceived the idea of incorporating the plan under Y.W.C.A. management, and the work has grown continuously. In Topeka last year (1938-9), 500 women were enrolled under 14 teachers. There were married women, business girls, high school girls, colored women and even a few men. The classes meet on weekdays or nights in different parts of the city, and there are numerous classes in other Kansas towns.

Each year I try to make the closing day finer than the last, if possible, and when the luncheon hour comes with from three to five hundred of my women about the tables and I go from one to the other until I have shaken every hand and spoken every name, I feel as if I could ask for no greater joy. And in the evening when I see them, all in simple white, file down the long aisle of the Woman's Club, and by classes, fill the platform to overflowing to testify to the fact that they have studied their Bibles for four years, thirty weeks a year, and receive their recognition certificate and pin, then I am sure no effort made or time spent was too hard or too much.

My aim in this Bible Class work has always been to make the Bible characters live, to make the Book itself understandable and interesting to the reader. I feel that we should view the text historically, symbolically, spiritually. I am sure it offers the best possible help to those who want to find God in their daily lives.

Chapter 21

IT is always beautiful at Oakwood, summer or winter, sunshine or rain, warm or cold. The autumns are often brilliant with color as the leaves in the grove yield to Jack Frost. In the winter when the trees are bare, we love to see the open spaces all about us, and the homes of our neighbors. In summer we live in the woods among the trees, and though warm at times, Oakwood is always cooler than the city. But one must see it to know how lovely it really is.

I think we have grown nearly everything in our garden that can be found in Kansas anywhere. Before the snow is off the ground the vegetable garden is a scene of activity, and the acres devoted to flowers have their share of attention with the first signs of spring. The thrill of getting things fresh from our own garden never grows old and I love to be out when the day is breaking to see the things that have really grown overnight. We have had all the kinds of berries and fruit that anyone could ask. Twenty varieties of lilac bushes overhang our driveway. The peony harvest has always been a great event in our lives. The rose gardens, the dahlias, the rare plants in the rock garden, the heavy burden

302

of the grape vines, the cherry trees laden with fruit, the apples begging to be picked, the grove of oak trees that gave our home its name and encouraged us to live much of the time out-of-doors under their beneficent shade—these things have been the soul of Oakwood to us.

Of course, Doctor's heart is with the flowers; from the earliest crocus to the last chrysanthemum in the fall—he loves them all. I think he has seen every bud that ever opened on the place, and the miles he has walked over the same paths to watch a bud open, to put a label on every plant, to catch the latest blossom, to name the newest variety! He has made us all love the flowers, though we are not as good as he at remembering the names.

No one could walk in the garden with Doctor and remain unimpressed by his vast knowledge of flowers and his great love for them. Sometimes I think there are degrees in his appreciation of the blooms, but as he starts with superlatives, no flower is slighted. *"This,"* he will say, "is positively beautiful; *that* is a little finer—but *here* is the finest thing in the garden!" Lilacs, peonies, poppies, iris, roses, dahlias, chrysanthemums! "I can hear what they say," he explains.

And can any visitor to Oakwood ever forget the inviting old "wheelbarrow seat" that has long held the place of honor in our back yard? Only a careless passer-by could miss the words that grace the highest board of its back support. The last verse of Gurney's

"The Lord God Planted a Garden" was surely meant for Oakwood:

> The kiss of the sun for pardon
> The song of the birds for mirth—
> One is nearer God's heart in a garden
> Than anywhere else on earth.

Much as I used to enjoy the noise and bustle of activity at 1251, now I love only its memories and its benedictions. I feel that God was good to Doctor and me to permit us the privilege of enjoying the beauty, the peace and the quiet of a home we built in our dreams so long ago. It has been unlimited pleasure to have our friends share the beauty of Oakwood with us, and it has meant much to us and to them—the quiet times with a few, the livelier times with larger groups from church, school and Horticultural Society. All these have added to our joy.

There have been many "family occasions" at Oakwood—holidays, birthdays, Sunday evenings, and of course Thanksgiving. We gather around the big table in the dining room, or have a picnic in the grove, or a supper in the summer house. The jollity that precedes and the quiet talk and the singing which usually follow are those of any happy family reunion.

And Christmas, the gladdest day of all the year! It begins with "Merry Christmas" on the telephone to all the children and grandchildren here, an exchange of telegrams with Florida, and then a Christmas visit to the homes of Karl, Will, and the Boams

Golden Wedding. January 15, 1935

to see and hear the children greet their Santa Claus. Late in the afternoon they all come to Oakwood. Of course, we must have all the Christmas decorations, including a tree. A fire in the grate adds cheer and brightness to an already delightful scene. After the Christmas story, Santa Claus distributes the presents from about the tree. Then we have our Christmas supper together, and sing some songs, and one after another they all go home. While Edwin, Jr. and Pearl busy themselves putting things away, my husband and I sit by the fire and think back over the many occasions in our lives that are now being re-enacted by new generations. We recall our first Christmas together in the little cottage at 1270 Topeka Avenue when I sang

> Hang up the baby's stocking
> And be sure you don't forget . . .

and later when I had to read over and over to three eager listeners "'Twas the Night Before Christmas." After a while their places were taken by others, first Julia, then Edwin, Jr. and Robert, then Barbara, Martha, Roy, Philip and Walter—in that order. With them, too, came Pearl and her brother Ben's family with Clarence, Josephine, Edna Lucille and Jack.

Red ashes turn to gray, and I think I can see far ahead when these children will be "mamma" and "papa" to other little children who watch for Santa Claus and say "Merry Christmas" just as we have done through many happy years. We know we shall live on and on in the hearts and lives of those who follow us and those whom we have loved. I hope their interest in the Christmas season will never abate, nor their faith in a Christ who came to teach men how to live. How wonderful it all is, this Christmas story of a mother and a babe in the manger, begun so long ago!

One of our very happiest days was January 15, 1935, our fiftieth wedding anniversary. It was scheduled to be a typically busy day—Bible class, Building and Loan Association meeting and a special meeting of the Horticultural Society. William Claire was to be in Chicago and Edwin, of course, was in Florida. So I had not thought of the day as any different from the many other anniversaries that had preceded it.

But Pearl and Grace and Catharine mentioned the anniversary several times and finally, a few days before, they said, "Now, mother, what are we going to do about this? If we are to have a reception, we must get the announcement in the papers." I said, "All right, do whatever you'd like to do." Preparations started at once.

Pearl suggested that I get down my "old medal chest" and select from it something to give to each of the children on Monday evening, when we were to have dinner with Karl and Grace. On Saturday evening, we loaded the table with *old* things of all sorts, and Grace came over Sunday afternoon to see what use could be made of them. She selected various old pictures, gowns and keepsakes, and she took my grandmother's spinning wheel and reel to adorn the fireplace. After supper, Karl phoned that he was coming to visit with us for a little while, and he brought William Claire, who had come in from Chicago to be with us for the anniversary.

On Monday morning everyone went to work as usual. I spent the forenoon studying Isaiah, and when Pearl came home from school she said we must all dress up just as if we were going to a big party. With my hair specially fixed, my new dress, and with Doctor in his dinner jacket and a silk top hat, our arrival at Karl's house created a real sensation. The children had never seen their grandfather in that hat, and their jollity was a good beginning for the evening's pleasure. Grace at once decided that she would put on her best dress; then the children urged Karl to change his clothes, which he did. All dressed up just to stay at home! It did not take long for the four youngsters to point out just where our efforts were successful and where they had failed.

Suddenly we heard the bang of a car door, three yells like a war cry, and the door burst open as three little boys, Roy, Philip and Walter came racing in, each one trying to make the most noise. And close at their heels was Edwin—Edwin all the way from Florida! William Claire and Catharine had brought him over. Such a surprise was truly one of life's greatest moments. They said I shouted, and the children wanted me to do it all over again.

We had a wonderful dinner. Grace knew what the
boys had liked to eat when they were at home together, and she had planned accordingly. There were
golden yellow candles, yellow flowers, beautiful
dishes—everything was perfect. We lingered around
the table a long time reminiscing about all the things
that had taken place in the fifty years. One of the
boys read the story of our wedding fifty years ago as
I had written it in this manuscript. Edwin remarked
that it had been twenty-one years since all three
brothers had been together, back in 1914 at Buffalo
Park, Colorado, but to me it seemed as if they had
never separated. The supreme moment of the day
came when Doctor and the boys gathered around the
piano and sang, sang the old songs just as they had
around the old red piano at 1251. I have always
loved to hear them sing.

On Tuesday, January 15, I taught my Bible
classes as usual, and at three o'clock, I found Doctor
waiting for me. We went home to a house very different than usual. There were folks in the kitchen
whipping cream, fixing chicken, wiping plates. The
front rooms had been turned into a bower of flowers
and there were lights and beauty everywhere—but
outdoors it was rather discouraging. For a week the
weather had been cloudy, foggy and rainy by turns.
In the morning it had grown colder and misty, and
then it began to rain and it rained all day. About
five o'clock it began to freeze, and the weather got
thicker as the night came on. It was rather a dis-

couraging outlook for a reception three miles out in the country.

But at four o'clock friends began to arrive and they continued to come until about six thirty, when there was a lull. As traveling was so bad, we felt there would be no more, but after seven, other groups arrived until altogether more than two hundred persons had called to honor the occasion.

It was a great pleasure to see the friends who came to wish us well, pleasant to recall with them the things that had been part of our lives in the old days. I hope that other couples who have the privilege of fifty years of life together will have the added blessing of loving children to make their golden wedding anniversary as happy as our children made ours.

Dreams are a common indulgence. Some dreams are fantastic and futile, but others are well founded and become sound ambitions. They urge us to follow our purpose with faith, in the belief that we can do whatever we want to do if we think we can. There are many obstacles to be overcome, and many of them we cannot understand, but holding fast to a purpose wins. We can do the thing we want to do if we are earnest enough to make it the first and greatest object in life. I have never found it hard to believe that there is a God who rules the universe, and that He is the power and strength that man can have if he believes and trusts Him. But how to live according to this belief—that has been my daily problem. How well I have succeeded remains to be told by my own family and by those who have tried to think with me as we have studied our Bibles through together. The whole New Testament tells us about a way of life that cannot fail to help anyone who accepts the pattern. "I am come that ye might have life, through His name." Those who have tried this believe it, and by their living help others to a happier life.